CW01654638

The Hertford Loop

Cover photograph:
Great Northern Railway trains at Palmers Green after the opening of the Cuffley extension in 1910.

THE HERTFORD LOOP

The First Hundred Years of a Local Railway

by Peter Hodge

SOUTHGATE CIVIC TRUST
1976

SOUTHGATE CIVIC TRUST
Honorary Secretary
70 *Vicars Moor Lane, London N21*

ISBN 0 905494 00 8

Printed in Great Britain by
Collins & Wilson Ltd, London and Andover

Preface

THIS BOOKLET has its origins in an article which appeared in the *Palmers Green and Southgate Gazette* and the *Enfield Gazette and Observer* in April 1971 to mark the centenary of the opening of the Great Northern Railway branch line from Wood Green to Enfield. It is an account, for the general reader, of the construction of the railway, its development into what is now the Hertford Loop, and the effect it has had on the localities it serves. Much could, and I hope one day will, be written on the legislative background to the construction of the line, and the technical aspects of its building and operation. Purposely I have made only passing reference to these matters, partly in the belief that they may be of rather specialist interest, but more particularly because there are others better qualified than myself to describe them. I hope readers will forgive me if, because this is a publication of the Southgate Civic Trust, there is more than due emphasis on events in Palmers Green and Winchmore Hill.

Publication of this booklet would not have been possible without generous financial backing from the London Borough of Enfield Arts Council, nor without the valuable help and advice reeeived from Southgate Civic Trust members. A special word of thanks is due to David Toy, Secretary of the Trust, who has undertaken the design and typography. I am also grateful to John Rowe, a member of Edmonton Hundred Historical Society, for advice and information provided in the preparation of parts of the text.

The pictures taken at Palmers Green are reproduced with kind permission of Real Photographs Ltd; the photograph of Winchmore Hill Station in 1902 comes from the Southgate Civic Trust local history collection; the remaining photographs are from the collection of the London Borough of Enfield Libraries, to whom I owe my grateful thanks.

Finally, I should mention that at the time of writing work was nearing completion on the electrification of this railway. If, as a result, some information in this booklet has been overtaken by events by the time it appears in print, I offer the reader my apologies.

Winchmore Hill, London
May 1976

Peter Hodge

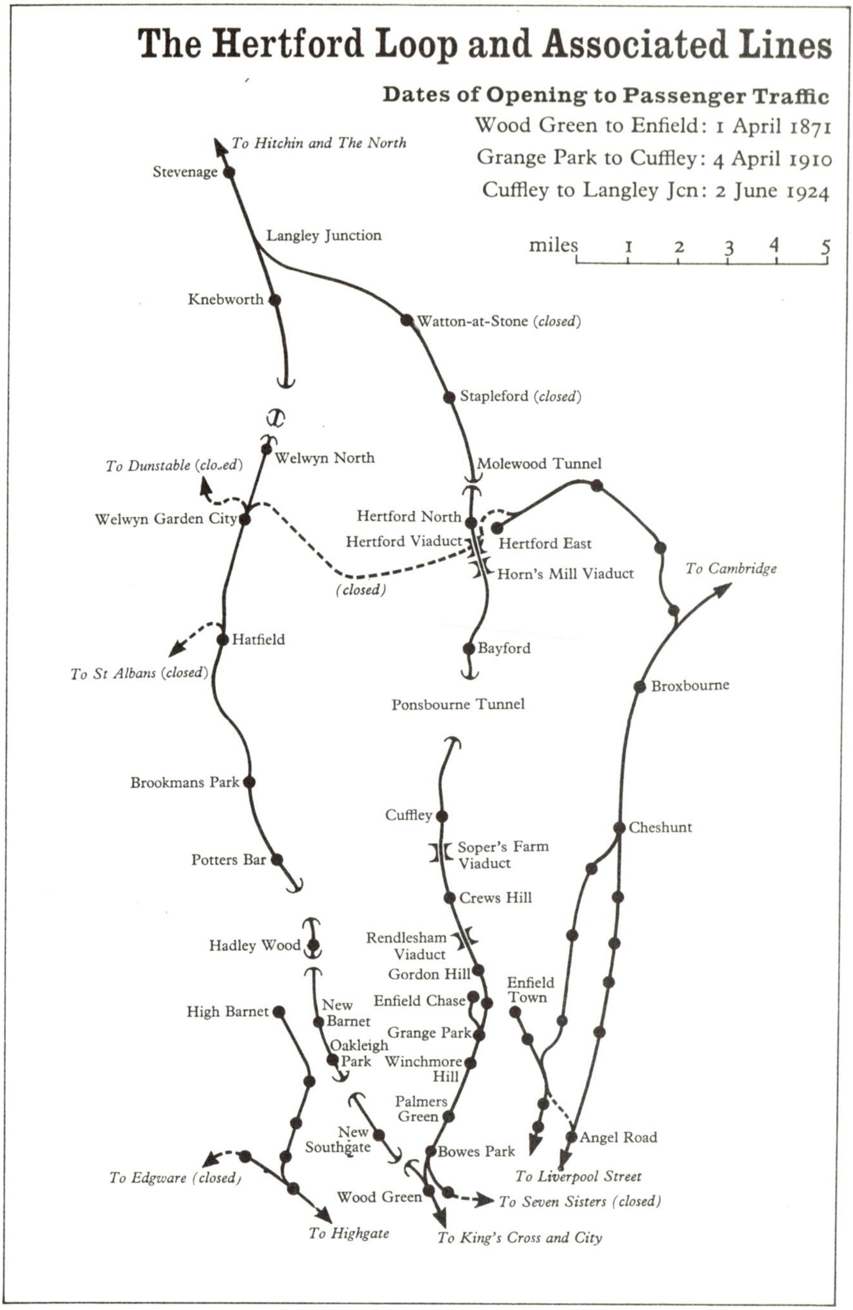
The Hertford Loop and Associated Lines
Dates of Opening to Passenger Traffic
Wood Green to Enfield: 1 April 1871
Grange Park to Cuffley: 4 April 1910
Cuffley to Langley Jcn: 2 June 1924
miles 1 2 3 4 5
To Hitchin and The North
Stevenage
Langley Junction
Knebworth
Watton-at-Stone (closed)
Stapleford (closed)
Welwyn North
To Dunstable (closed)
Molewood Tunnel
Welwyn Garden City
Hertford North
Hertford Viaduct
Hertford East
Horn's Mill Viaduct
To Cambridge
(closed)
Hatfield
Bayford
To St Albans (closed)
Broxbourne
Ponsbourne Tunnel
Brookmans Park
Cuffley
Cheshunt
Soper's Farm Viaduct
Potters Bar
Crews Hill
Hadley Wood
Rendlesham Viaduct
Gordon Hill
Enfield Town
New Barnet
Enfield Chase
High Barnet
Grange Park
Oakleigh Park
Winchmore Hill
Palmers Green
New Southgate
Angel Road
Bowes Park
To Edgware (closed)
To Liverpool Street
Wood Green
To Seven Sisters (closed)
To Highgate
To King's Cross and City

AMONG the thousands of commuters who daily flock into and out of London by train, there will be few who have given much thought to how their local railway came to be built, or to how its existence has influenced the growth of the residential suburbs in which they live. Yet the spread of suburban London in the 19th century was closely interwoven with the expansion of the railway system, and the pattern of development has been both cause and effect of the provision of suburban railway services. By looking at the case of our own local railway we may observe this process in microcosm.

Railway expansion in 19th century London was geographically unbalanced. The first line was the London and Greenwich, opened in 1836, and this was to become part of the dense network of suburban railways which grew up south of the Thames. The principal main line companies running into London on the north side were, however, preoccupied with their more profitable long distance traffic, and they tended to neglect suburban traffic in the early years. To this the Great Northern Railway was no exception. Its main line from Doncaster to King's Cross was completed in 1852, and although stations were opened near London at Hornsey, Colney Hatch, Barnet and Potters Bar, these were slow in attracting traffic. Only in the late 1860s did building development begin to take place north of Holloway, and even in 1870 there were still open fields between Finsbury Park and Wood Green. In these circumstances it may seem surprising that in 1869 the Great Northern Railway should begin construction of a four mile branch line from Wood Green, on its main line from King's Cross, to the market town of Enfield.

Great Northern to Enfield

Superficially, the promotion of the Wood Green – Enfield branch line at this time appears surprising for two reasons: one that it would traverse an area offering little potential for traffic growth; the other that Enfield was already rail connected. The intervening country through which the line would pass, taking in the villages of Palmers Green and Winchmore Hill, and the adjacent village of Southgate, was at the time thinly populated and undeveloped, its clay soil encouraging neither agriculture nor building. Miss Henrietta Cresswell, daughter of the village doctor at Winchmore Hill when the line was built, tells us that:

> There were at that time no houses between Winchmore Hill and Wood Green, except the old cottages on or near the high road, Palmerston Villas, and a few gentlemen's houses in their own grounds, and no part of West Enfield was built with the exception of a few large villas on the Ridge Way.

Enfield itself, which was already a flourishing market town with a population of about 16,000, had been put on the railway map in 1849, when a branch line was opened from the station at Water Lane, Edmonton (later Angel Road) on the Cambridge main line of the Eastern Counties Railway. In 1862 this became part of the Great Eastern Railway, and that company's policy of providing workmen's trains at very low fares encouraged the development of eastern Enfield as a working class district during the 1860s and 1870s, in common with other North East London suburbs.

Although the Great Northern Railway could see potential suburban growth in the Enfield area, its main justification for projecting the line towards Enfield was to provide an alternative route for main line trains. There were, on the Great Northern main line near London, several tunnels, and at Welwyn a large viaduct, which would have made any widening of that line very costly. But during the 1860s main line traffic was increasing to such an extent that the company was obliged to seek some relief, especially as trains of the Midland Railway also ran over the GNR main line between Hitchin and King's Cross until the opening of the extension into St Pancras in 1868. Consequently, the GNR sought to construct a loop line from Wood Green, through Enfield, to Hertford, where a connection would be made to the Hertford and Welwyn line (opened in 1858), enabling main line trains to regain their former route near Welwyn. The proposed line was referred to as the 'Hornsey and Hertford Railway'.

Parliamentary powers were obtained for this scheme in 1865. In the previous year, authority had been sought by an independent company for the construction of a Wood Green and Enfield Railway, which would have followed a similar route to the Hornsey and Hertford as far as Palmers Green, continuing from there to a junction with the Enfield Town branch of the GER and then on to join the Cambridge main line at Ordnance Factory Station (later Enfield Lock). This abortive proposal appears to have prompted the GNR's desire to have its own route to Enfield, and therefore it is perhaps not so surprising that in 1869, the year in which construction of the Wood Green – Enfield section of the GNR line began, the powers for the section from Enfield to Hertford were abandoned in the aftermath of the 1866 financial crisis. Thus the project became a purely local branch line scheme even before its opening.

It is well to remember that by the late 1860s conditions were changing in favour of the development of suburban rail traffic. Slowly, small built up areas were appearing around the stations on the GNR main line out towards Barnet, and the opening of a branch line from Seven Sisters Road (later Finsbury Park) in 1867, to serve the expanding communities of Highgate, Finchley and Edgware, provided a further stimulus to suburban traffic. In the following year, the GNR gained access to the City for its suburban trains with the opening by the Metropolitan Railway of the Widened Lines, paralleling that company's existing route between

King's Cross and Moorgate Street, and this paved the way for intensive residential services to City stations from suburbs served by the GNR. Altogether, therefore, circumstances were not unfavourable to the promotion of the Enfield line as a suburban branch by the time it came to be built.

Among all the accounts of 19th century railway building, there can be few which describe in such vivid detail the appearance of the construction works, and their effect on the local community, as that written by Miss Cresswell of the section of the Enfield branch line which passed through her own village of Winchmore Hill. Miss Cresswell's reminiscences of this quiet Middlesex village, written more than 30 years after the opening of the line, give a clear indication of the impact which the coming of the railway must have had on a young impressionable mind.

She recalls how the peace of the village was shattered in the summer of 1869 by the arrival of the railway contractors, and how within a few days the navvies' wooden huts appeared – 'mushroom-like' – on the site of the excavations. But the upheaval had its compensations:

> The excavations were beautiful in colour, the London clay being a bright cobalt blue when first cut through, and changing with exposure to orange. There were strata of black and white flints and yellow gravel; the men's white slops, and the red heaps of burnt ballast made vivid effects of light and shade against the cloudless sky of that excessively hot summer. There were also dark wooden planks and shorings to add neutral tints, and when the engine came the glitter of brass and clouds of white steam were added to the landscape. On Sundays and holidays the men were, many of them, resplendent in scarlet or yellow or blue plush waistcoats and knee breeches.

Apparently the navvies were, on the whole, respectable and well mannered – a picture which does not correspond with the typical impression of riotous and drunken behaviour associated with railway construction.

In the disturbance caused to property, however, the building of the railway in Winchmore Hill followed the all too familiar pattern – houses demolished, gardens devastated, and quiet corners abandoned to noise and destruction. Between the skew bridge on Hoppers Road and Vicars Moor Lane the railway sliced through the heart of the old village; among the casualties were an Independent Chapel, several large houses (one of which was occupied by Dr Cresswell) and a row of cottages. No amenity society existed then to argue the case for preservation!

Nature scored one small victory over the railway. Between Winchmore Hill and Enfield the line had to cross the valley through which Salmon's Brook and Houndsden Gutter flow to their confluence near what is now Grange Park:

> The great business was the spanning of the deep valley between the village and the hills to the North. The summer was one of heat and drought, the stream was nearly dry, and the engineers took an entirely erroneous view of its capabilities: they did not realise the extent of the watershed from the hills on either side, and when the inhabitants described 'lakes of flood water, and bridges washed away and piled one upon another' they were listened to in polite disbelief.

Through either miscalculation or bad luck, the winter rains cracked a culvert carrying one of the streams through the railway embankment, and the soft clay subsided, causing the embankment to slip. Bad weather also hindered construction of the stations, and the opening of the line was delayed several weeks, finally taking place on 1st April 1871. Even after the opening the embankment gave trouble, and a slip remained in the line north of Winchmore Hill. Some timorous passengers, we are told, were uncertain for a time that it was safe to travel by train to Enfield!

The choice of All Fools' Day for the opening of the line was greeted with some mirth by local people. Nevertheless, the inaugural train ran without incident or ceremony, although the previous night the navvies had celebrated their departure from Winchmore Hill with the explosion of a quantity of fog detonators under the railway bridge – the cause of much consternation in the village until the source of the noise was discovered. The new line had three stations: Palmers Green, Winchmore Hill and Enfield. Five workmen had lost their lives during its construction.

It is difficult to visualise today the significance which the construction of a railway must have had to an isolated village community like Winchmore Hill in the second half of the 19th century. Though only 10 miles from London, Winchmore Hill would have been very self contained before the coming of the railway. Undoubtedly there were people who made the daily journey to town, but they would have been a small minority. The only means of communication with the outside world, for those who did not have their own carriages, were the four daily horse buses, two from the King's Head on Winchmore Hill Green to the Flower Pot in Bishopsgate, and two from the Green Dragon to London Bridge. But the

Exterior of the original terminus of the Enfield branch on Windmill Hill, Enfield. This was closed in 1910 *when the line was extended to Cuffley.*

journey could take anything up to two hours. The alternative, which was apparently adopted by some people, was to walk to the nearest railway station – either Edmonton or Wood Green. But either way the journey would have been an arduous one, particularly in winter. The residents of Southgate were rather more fortunate, for they had a horse bus connecting with the GNR trains at Colney Hatch Station (now New Southgate).

All this was changed by the new railway. The improvements in speed and comfort which it brought made a daily journey to and from London a reasonable proposition for many people for the first time, and during the 1880s Palmers Green Station in particular developed into what we would now call a 'commuter railhead', drawing much of its traffic from the Southgate area. The Southgate horse bus was diverted from Colney Hatch to Palmers Green, and some of the wealthier citizens were driven to the station in their own carriages.

A clear illustration of how the railway enlarged the scope of people's lives was the way in which it created new opportunities for the enjoyment of leisure by providing cheap and convenient transport to a wide range of entertainments, social events and sporting activities. Very soon after the line was opened, for example, large numbers of people arrived at Enfield by train to attend the newly instituted steeplechases held annually in the grounds of Bycullah Park. London theatregoers were catered for by a late train which ran on Wednesday and Friday evenings from King's Cross to Hatfield, a portion being detached at Wood Green and arriving at Enfield shortly before 1 am. The annual Sunday school treat, already a well established feature of village life, became a more ambitious affair, so much so that in 1892 the Winchmore Hill Sunday School seaside outing finished in a lively mood on the last train at 12.14 am, and the Vicar resolved 'never to allow such a dissipation under the name of a treat to happen again'. In the same year, Sir Thomas Lipton moved to his Southgate home at 'Osidge', and arranged an annual garden party in his grounds for the staff at Lipton's. In 1897 he hired a special train from Moorgate Street to Palmers Green to bring his guests to this event, and had them met at the station with private carriages. Such were a few of the purposes for which the railway was used in the early years.

What would it have been like to travel on the railway in those early days? Possibly one of the more striking features to our eyes, at least in the first few years, would have been the stark appearance of the newly excavated cuttings and embankments. Today we are used to seeing these in a mature state, overgrown with grass and foliage; in 1871, little but bare clay would have been visible. The stations at Palmers Green and Winchmore Hill remained little changed during their first hundred years, but their gaslit platforms had a less ordered appearance in Victorian times, suffering from the untidy proliferation of advertising associated with late 19th century railway stations. Gas lighting survived at these stations until the early 1960s.

The first trains to run on the line consisted of uncomfortable four-wheeled carriages hauled by small tank engines, in comparison with which modern rolling stock would seem quite luxurious. First, second and third class accommodation was provided (first class did not disappear until the last war), and a local railway journey was altogether a more leisurely experience than it is today. By present day standards the trains were slow and infrequent. The inaugural service consisted of only 16 Up and 15 Down trains a day on weekdays, and five each way on Sundays; even until the early years of the present century it was not the practice to run trains during churchgoing hours on Sunday mornings. To support this modest service, stations were lavishly staffed. At Winchmore Hill, for example, there was a station master, a booking clerk, two signalmen and a porter.

Villages into Suburbs

Despite the modernising influence of the railway, the villages between Wood Green and Enfield were slow to develop into heavily populated suburbs. In 1876 James Thorne described Palmers Green as 'a little gathering of houses on the road to Enfield' (the station was still almost surrounded by open fields in the mid-1880s), and of Winchmore Hill he wrote:

The country hereabouts is undulating, abundantly wooded, and agreeable, and it has long been a favourite residence with City men, whose comfortable houses are seen on every hand.

For more than 30 years after its opening, Winchmore Hill Station was approached along a country lane; this did not acquire the name Station Road until 1902. Southgate was similarly unaffected by building development, except for the erection of a few houses in the Chase Side area, and together with Winchmore Hill retained its rural atmosphere well into the present century. This slow beginning was due very largely to the unwillingness of influential landowners to dispose of their property. Prominent among these was John Donnithorne Taylor, two of whose estates were pierced by the railway – Grovelands, between Southgate and Winchmore Hill, and Old Park, on which Palmers Green Station was built. Taylor insisted on the construction of a private bridge over the line at Winchmore Hill (since removed) to give his farmcarts access to Hoppers Road, and he is believed to have had a financial interest in a horse bus service to the City which ran in competition with the railway until 1879. The Walker family, of Southgate, went so far as to create their own private 'green belt' as a barrier against the encroachment of suburban development at a time when other districts a similar distance from London were becoming completely built up, and this policy proved successful until the early years of the present century.

While Palmers Green, Winchmore Hill and Southgate remained rural backwaters, however, the districts at each end of the line – the northern part of Wood Green and western Enfield – did develop when the pace of building began to quicken in the late 1870s and during the 1880s. Bowes Park, north of Wood Green, soon became built up, mostly with small terrace houses, and in 1880 a station was opened to serve the area. At the other end of the line, Enfield spread westwards with the development of the Chase Side and Lancaster Road areas, and the building of better class houses in the grounds of Bycullah Park. This helped to balance the extensive working class development which had taken place in eastern Enfield a decade or so earlier. The population of Enfield grew from 16,000 in 1871 to 19,000 in 1881; by 1891 it was nearly 32,000.

Only during the first decade of the present century did development begin in earnest at Palmers Green and Winchmore Hill, when land prices had risen sufficiently to encourage formerly tenacious landowners to dispose of their properties. On 4th May 1902, for example, an advertisement appeared in Palmers Green for:

A highly important and valuable freehold building estate . . . with extensive frontages to the main roads known as Fox Lane and Dog and Duck Lane being ripe for immediate development and possession on completion of purchase . . . situate 500 yds. from Palmers Green Station, and 15 minutes' walk from Winchmore Hill Station, both on the Enfield branch of the Great Northern Railway, with frequent service to Broad Street, Moorgate Street and King's Cross.

Winchmore Hill did not succumb quite so soon, the population by 1906 being less than 5,000. A residential property guide published in that year, however, included the following information:

A large number of well-designed modern residences have been erected on the outskirts of the old village during the last two or three years . . . There are plenty of quick trains on the Great Northern Railway to or from King's Cross and the City, and local travelling facilities will be usefully increased in a few months time by a line of electric tramways.

The electric tramway, which reached Winchmore Hill two years later, accelerated the process of building development in both Palmers Green and Winchmore Hill.

While the streets of Edwardian villas were going up in Palmers Green, an ambitious experiment in town planning was being considered for Winchmore Hill, in which the railway station would have featured prominently. In October 1909, under the heading 'A Beautiful Woodland City', the *Recorder for Palmers Green,*

Enfield train entering Winchmore Hill Station in July 1902. The station was decorated for the wedding of the Vicar of St Paul's, Winchmore Hill.

Winchmore Hill and Southgate reported plans for the development of Winchmore Hill Woods and the Grovelands Estate, which, if carried out, 'will not only be unique in this country, but will be a model for all Europe'. The idea was to lay out a spacious estate of detached houses in a landscaped setting, preserving as many of the trees as possible, and turning part of Grovelands into a private park for the residents. The aim of the promoters was 'to build an Englishman's ideal home':

> With the exception of the great drive through the woods from Winchmore Hill to Bourne Hill there is not a straight road on the estate. All are gracefully curved and lead on to a magnificent business thoroughfare as wide as Kingsway, terminating in a fine circus, which is flanked by a new railway station . . . In the centre of the estate will be a road, which will lead directly to the new station, which will ultimately be built on the spot in Hoppers Road where the line passes in close parallel to the roadway . . . In front of the railway station will be a fine half circus, flanked by shops, and containing in the centre a plantation of trees. Straight ahead in a westerly direction fine shops will stand on each side of a 100-ft. roadway, containing pavements 15 ft. wide.

The proposal to move the station met with strong opposition from local traders, who feared that business would be taken away from the old village centre. As it turned out, nothing was done, either to move the station, or to build the estate on the lines envisaged. Instead, the streets in the vicinity of Winchmore Hill Station developed in much the same way as they had done at Palmers Green, although some of the features of the 'Woodland City' did appear later when 'the great drive through the woods' became Broad Walk. An interesting, but short lived, proposal connected with the development of the Grovelands Estate was to build a light railway from Winchmore Hill to Oakleigh Park and New Barnet, thus linking the Enfield branch with the GNR main line.

The GNR, eager to take advantage of the attractions of the new suburbs to increase its traffic, began intensive publicity to encourage people to live in the areas served by its trains. 'Exchange fog for sunshine', exhorted a poster of 1906, highlighting the advantages of living in the districts along the Enfield branch and the Northern Heights lines, 'Compare London's rents and taxes with those in the suburbs. Frequent trains and cheap rates make it possible to combine the pleasures of the country with the privileges of town. The railway company will give every assistance to those seeking healthy homes'. The company also published, every quarter, a guide entitled *Where to Live,* which gave in more detail information about the Great Northern suburbs. The first issue for 1910 contained more than 100 pages of descriptive matter and photographs, many of them of Palmers Green, Southgate and Winchmore Hill, and referred in detail to the proposed 'Woodland City' scheme. Despite some over glamourised descriptions and a few historical inaccuracies, the book appears to have painted an attractive picture of the neighbourhood.

With the encouragement given to suburban development in Palmers Green and Winchmore Hill, and the continued growth in traffic at Enfield, the GNR was faced with new demands on the Enfield branch. Although no general scheme of improvements was carried out at this time, some minor works were undertaken. At Palmers Green, for example, worn stairways were renewed, and a more substantial ticket collector's hut was built on the Down platform. One innovation which was not welcomed was the provision of a gate at the top of the stairs on the Up side, to prevent passengers from delaying morning trains by running for them at the last minute. This provoked angry reactions from tardy City businessmen who suffered the indignity of having the gate shut in their faces.

During this period, the railway was a frequent topic of news in the district. The local press referred often to fares and standards of service, and periodically the GNR was urged, through the correspondence columns, to pay greater attention to the needs of its customers. One of the more unusual pleas came in 1911 from a Palmers Green resident who objected to the threatened withdrawal of the 2.59 am train to London: 'Having a train at such an early hour must be a great boon to residents who are employed in the London markets, &c., and whose business necessitates their being in town at an early hour'. Railway users did not restrict their criticisms to the company; sometimes they complained about the behaviour of their fellow travellers. In 1909, for example, a correspondent from Winchmore Hill, irritated by the incessant conversation of certain other passengers, suggested that the railway company might 'affix labels to reserved carriages where these lunatics can talk about their gardens and their feats of bowling without annoying other passengers who want to read their half-penny morning papers'.

Although the railway company, and some of its customers, were targets for criticism, the railway staff appear to have received more sympathetic treatment. Probably the most highly respected railway servant was the local station master, who had been a figure of importance in the community since the opening of the line. He provided a link between the large, impersonal railway company and the everyday lives of the local people, and the company's reputation depended very much on his ability. In 1912, the residents of Winchmore Hill made a presentation to their station master, who was emigrating to Australia after 12 years' service. In the presence of local dignitaries and well wishers he was handed an illuminated address:

> Presented to Mr. Charles Randall, Stationmaster of Winchmore Hill, in the County of Middlesex. This Testimonial, together with a purse containing a sum of £50, was, on the 31st day of May, 1912, presented at St. Paul's Institute, by W. T. Paulin, Esq., J.P., on behalf of the residents, to mark their appreciation of his faithful, effective, and courteous service as Stationmaster, from 1900 to 1912.

The event was clearly one of importance in the life of the district. Public gratitude appears also to have extended to the lower grades of staff, a local resident sympathising in 1911 with the porters at Palmers Green Station, whose arduous duties included 'the carrying of 30 full milk churns each morning, the cleaning of windows, &c., the scrubbing of floors, the black-leading of fire-grates, the checking of parcels, attending to luggage, and a thousand and one odd duties' – all for a wage of 17 to 18 shillings a week.

By this time, the GNR had built up a substantial suburban traffic on all its London area routes, including the Enfield line. So successful had it been in this respect that the volume of traffic was beginning to place a severe strain on the company's resources. Not that this was anything new: ever since the 1870s the GNR had been trying to find additional capacity for its growing suburban traffic. Soon after the opening of the Enfield branch, for example, the company had approached the North London Railway with a view to obtaining running powers into Broad Street Station over the connection between Finsbury Park and Canonbury Junction, thereby securing an alternative route to the City. This approach was unsuccessful, however, and the GNR was instead obliged to invite the North London to run its own trains from Broad Street over GNR lines, an arrangement which began in 1875, when the Enfield service (among others) was supplemented by NLR trains.

Also in 1875, the GNR had opened the suburban station at King's Cross. This provided much needed additional platform capacity, and avoided the necessity for trains from Moorgate Street to reverse into King's Cross main line station. A further measure undertaken to relieve congestion at this time was the widening of Copenhagen and Maiden Lane (later Gasworks) Tunnels, at the approaches to King's Cross, in 1877-78. These improvements barely kept pace with the growth in traffic, however, the 69 suburban departures a day from King's Cross in 1873 having grown to 128 by 1893. On the Enfield branch, the original service of 15-16 trains a day had grown to nearly 30 by 1880. Thereafter the service had continued to expand in response to the growth in population towards the end of the century, and by 1903 there were as many as 55 trains in each direction on weekdays, most of them running through between Enfield and the City termini. The trains ran at irregular intervals, the journey from Enfield to Moorgate Street taking 40-45 minutes. Cheap workmen's tickets were available on the early morning trains to town. For some years the service had included a few trains to and from stations on the South Eastern and London Chatham & Dover Railways. The July 1903 timetable, for example, shows four trains a day from Enfield to Victoria, and one from Enfield to Woolwich Arsenal, with return services from Victoria and Charlton Junction. These trains, which ran through London via King's Cross, Farringdon Street, Ludgate Hill and Blackfriars, were examples of the numerous cross-London steam suburban services of the period. Although they traversed circuitous routes (the journey from Enfield to Victoria took about 80 minutes), they provided useful cross-town links in the days before the more direct tube railways. By 1907 they had outlived their usefulness, and were withdrawn.

Although concerned with the need to provide additional capacity for suburban trains at this time, the GNR had not forgotten the problems which existed on its main line south of Hitchin, and which had given rise to the original proposal to build the Enfield branch as part of a through route for main line trains. As these problems grew towards the end of the century, further proposals were forthcoming which in time were to give the Enfield branch a new importance.

The Loop Completed

We have seen how the loop line originally proposed from Wood Green to Hertford was stopped short at Enfield, and how instead it came into being, and existed for many years, as a self contained branch line. One result of this truncation was that the Hertford and Welwyn line, which the extension from Enfield would have joined at Hertingfordbury, never acquired strategic importance as a through route. Unable to compete with the more convenient Great Eastern route to Hertford via Broxbourne, it settled down to a sleepy existence as a country branch line, its local passenger service lingering on until June 1951.

Having abandoned its original proposal to extend north of Enfield, the GNR turned its attention during the 1870s and 1880s to other ways of relieving main line congestion. The most obvious solution was to widen the main line itself, but major engineering works, and especially the viaduct at Welwyn, would have made this prohibitively expensive. An alternative proposal was to extend the High Barnet branch (opened in 1872) northwards to rejoin the main line, but this was a steeply graded route climbing up onto the Northern Heights from Finsbury Park, and would have been unsuitable for express trains. Other schemes were put forward for extending the Enfield branch northwards, and by 1895 these ideas had resolved themselves into the plan finally adopted, which was to extend the branch on through Hertford to a point on the main line just south of Stevenage. It was felt that this route would not only provide the necessary relief to the main line, but would also tap new sources of residential traffic north of Enfield.

The GNR obtained its Act for the extension in 1898, but work did not begin until 1906. To avoid the necessity for a level crossing over Windmill Hill, Enfield, a new line was constructed from a point south of the Enfield terminus to enable it to gain sufficient height before reaching Enfield to cross Windmill Hill on a bridge. Just south of the junction with the old line a new station, called Grange Park, was constructed to serve a developing residential area. Another new station was constructed at Enfield, on the south side of Windmill Hill, to replace the old terminal station (in 1923 the new station was renamed Enfield Chase to distinguish it from the former GER station, which was known as Enfield Town). The old GNR

Building the Cuffley extension, c. 1907, in the vicinity of Gordon Hill. North of Enfield the line was constructed through open country, much of which remains as part of the Green Belt.

terminus at Enfield was closed to passengers when the new line was opened, and subsequently became a goods depot. By 1910 the new line had reached Cuffley, and on 4th April the Enfield – Cuffley section was opened, with intermediate stations at Gordon Hill and Crews Hill. Two major civil engineering works on this section were Rendlesham Viaduct, spanning the valley between Gordon Hill and Crews Hill, and Soper's Farm Viaduct, between Crews Hill and Cuffley.

The extension opened with quiet efficiency. The first passenger from Enfield to Cuffley was the landlord of the Wheatsheaf on Windmill Hill, who was believed to have been the first passenger on the original Enfield branch almost 40 years previously. The *Enfield Observer* reported that during the first week 'a good number of passengers travelled to the new stations – more out of curiosity than anything else; and the general excellence of the Company's arrangements was favourably commented on'. It had been intended to run a shuttle service of steam railcars between Cuffley and Enfield, to connect with the London trains, but the GNR decided instead to run ordinary through trains to Cuffley, no doubt heartened by the prospect of residential development north of Enfield. As the *Enfield Observer* commented, shortly before the opening of the line:

> By completion of the Enfield – Cuffley line, the Great Northern Railway Co. opens up a district which has not hitherto been served by any railway. It is a fine open country, equally eligible for residential purposes as the picturesque district served by the Company's main line between New Southgate and Potters Bar.

Growing financial difficulties caused postponement of the continuation beyond Cuffley. As the *Railway Times* observed: 'It is, no doubt, unfortunate from the point of view of the running department that the Board do not feel justified in continuing the line at present; but the wisdom of a cautious policy in the present state of the money market is indisputable'. When work was resumed, further delay was incurred by the construction of Ponsbourne Tunnel and Horn's Mill and Hertford Viaducts, and by a shortage of labour and materials during the First World War. By March 1918, however, a single track was ready all the way from Cuffley, through Hertford, to Langley Junction, where the loop rejoined the main line south of Stevenage. Although there was no crossing loop for 15 miles on this single line, goods trains began using it. By the end of 1920 the double track was completed, but passenger trains did not start running north of Cuffley until 2nd June 1924, more than 25 years after the line had been authorised. By this time the GNR had been absorbed into the London and North Eastern Railway at the grouping of the main line railways in 1923. North of Cuffley new stations were opened at Bayford, Hertford (North), Stapleford and Watton-at-Stone. A station was also planned at Datchworth, between Watton and Stevenage, but never built. When Hertford North Station was opened, a connection was put in to the Welwyn line to enable the branch trains to use the station, and the old GNR terminus near the centre of Hertford was closed.

The Hertford Loop (known in railway circles as the New Line) proved its worth as a diversionary route for main line trains even before regular passenger services began running beyond Cuffley. In the early hours of 6th February 1920 two goods trains collided in Welwyn North Tunnel, blocking the main line from King's Cross to the North. Although the northern section of the Hertford Loop had not been officially inspected by the Ministry of Transport, the decision was taken to divert main line trains over it, and 26 trains, including a number of expresses, ran through via Enfield and Cuffley before the main line was reopened. Since then the route has proved invaluable for diversions, not only in emergencies, but also during periods of engineering work on the main line.

The usefulness of the Hertford Loop as an alternative through route was further increased after 1929, when a connection was put in between Bowes Park and Palace Gates to provide a new link with the former Great Eastern system via the branch line from Seven Sisters, opened in 1878. Although regular passenger trains never ran over this connection, it was extensively used by freight trains, and on occasions by excursions and diverted passenger trains. During 1947, for example, when the Liverpool Street–Cambridge main line was flooded at Tottenham, some trains ran from Liverpool Street to Cambridge via Seven Sisters, Palace Gates, Hertford North and Hitchin. This link was severed when the Seven Sisters–Palace Gates branch was closed.

Completion of the Hertford Loop was not however justified only by its value as a diversionary route. The expectation that local traffic would be attracted to the extension was soon realised, and several communities have developed since the railway was opened. The first of these was the Grange Estate, served by the new station at Grange Park. This estate, laid out by Messrs R. Metherell and Son of Winchmore Hill, took its name from the nearby Old Park Grange (formerly a hunting lodge in Enfield Chace), which had to be demolished to make way for the railway embankment between Grange Park and Enfield when the line was extended to Cuffley. Mr Metherell is reported to have suggested to the GNR himself that a new station should be erected to serve his estate, and he gave up to the railway company several acres of land for this purpose. Although completion of the station was originally planned for 1908, legal difficulties delayed its opening, and it was brought into use when the Cuffley extension was opened on 4th April 1910. In October of that year, the *Recorder* carried an article on the estate, under the heading 'Our Newest Suburb':

> A few days ago, writes a correspondent, I got out of the train at Grange Park station. I fancy I can hear some Palmers Green reader . . . asking 'Where's that?' Readers further afield may, perhaps, wonder more where the station is, for on looking through the 'A.B.C.' timetable there are five railway stations in this country the names of which begin with Grange. But there is only one Grange Park, and it is the newest station on the Great Northern Railway, lying between Winchmore Hill and Enfield . . . What is there in this new station that calls for more than a mere word of mention? It is high up on the embankment; it is more than that; it is the special station which adjoins what some people describe as an estate, but which I prefer to think of as the last word in residential city building.

The writer continues with a flattering description of the new development, praising its beautiful houses, well-lighted roads and attractive shopping centre – 'a city of health and beauty, which in the fulness of time will be one of the proudest possessions of our district'. Although perhaps falling a little short of the extravagant claims made for it, Grange Park did become an attractive residential area, and provided the GNR with a useful additional source of traffic.

The probability of residential development spreading north of Enfield after the opening of the railway extension was not attractive to Enfield's historian, C. W. Whitaker, who wrote in 1911:

The recent opening of the Great Northern Railway extension to Cuffley will probably lead to building developments in the near future, stations having been established at Gordon Hill and Crews Hill. The Chace will thus lose its rural aspect, after a century of cultivation, following upon several centuries of preservation for the chase, and will degenerate into 'crescents,' 'avenues,' and 'parades'.

Building certainly did take place in the northern part of Enfield, agricultural land being given over to housing in the Lavender Hill area. But the effect was not as widespread as Whitaker may have envisaged, for the built up area had not extended beyond Gordon Hill when the Green Belt legislation of 1938 checked further expansion northwards, and Crews Hill Station is still surrounded by nurseries and open fields. When the extension was first opened, Cuffley (formerly Coffleys) was a hamlet adjoining the small Hertfordshire village of Gough's (or Goff's) Oak, on the road from Cheshunt to Northaw, and few of the trains went beyond Gordon Hill. Today, Cuffley has become a modest dormitory settlement within the Green Belt. North of Cuffley the line still runs through an entirely rural countryside, except where it skirts the edge of Hertford.

The Busiest Years

During the first 30 years of the present century, while the extension was being planned, constructed and opened, the southern part of the Enfield branch was enjoying its heyday. The stations south of Gordon Hill attracted a high level of commuter traffic, which was catered for by an intensive passenger service. By 1914 this had reached about 70 trains in each direction on weekdays, some 20 of which served stations north of Gordon Hill. Suburban traffic continued to expand after the First World War, and the addition of the Hertford North services brought the number of trains in each direction up to 80 or more per day in the early 1930s. About half these trains started or terminated at Gordon Hill and about a quarter at Hertford North, the remainder running to or from Bowes Park, Grange Park and Cuffley. Reversal of trains at Bowes Park was a feature of the service which catered for the high level of short distance inner suburban traffic carried at the time.

The increasing volume of traffic in the early years of the century brought demands for improved rolling stock, and on 17th August 1911 the local press was able to report:

Passengers at Palmers Green Station last Thursday were surprised and even startled to see a brand-new train, consisting of about eight handsomely upholstered coaches, stop at the station between the hours of 3 and 4.30 and 5 and 6. A trial run of these new carriages was being made, and it is understood that this improved type of coach will shortly be used on this line by the Great Northern Company.

But while the GNR was apparently concerned for the comfort of its passengers, the old four-wheeled carriages used by the North London Railway on its Broad Street services were well below standard, and frequent complaints were made about such things as inadequate lighting and absence of luggage racks. These carriages were not replaced until after the First World War, by which time the GNR services were being taken over by new eight-coach trains hauled by a new design of 0-6-2 tank locomotive, both the work of H.N. (later Sir Nigel) Gresley.

The new trains, each made up of two four-coach articulated sets, were designed to provide maximum seating capacity in minimum length, and some continued in use until the mid-1960s. The Gresley locomotives, built in 1920-21, remained a familiar sight on the King's Cross suburban services until replaced by diesel traction in 1959.

Although commuter travel has always predominated on the Hertford Loop, the line has carried its share of recreational and pleasure traffic, and this was stimulated by the extension north of Enfield. During the summer of 1910, when the Cuffley extension was newly opened, Cuffley became a popular spot for excursions and picnics. A visitor to the area described the 'magnificent woodland, hills, valleys, and delightful views', and claimed that from the top of Carbone Hill he could see the Crystal Palace and the North Downs. Two years later, according to one correspondent, the area was becoming well known:

> Now that the long days of summer have arrived, half holidays and evenings in the country are more than ever enjoyable, and the short and pleasant trip to leafy Hertfordshire at Cuffley and Goff's Oak will be increasingly popular. The GNR branch to Cuffley, as most people know, though intended eventually to reach the main line at Stevenage, has its present terminus in the middle of a field – at first sight, at any rate, a very curious arrangement . . . It may be added that the picturesque scenery of Hertfordshire, and the pleasant undulating and varied character of the country is very attractive, and most people who have been there once want to go there again.

A North London Railway train from Broad Street to Enfield at Palmers Green around the First World War period. The through service from Broad Street started in 1875.

Cuffley provided an attraction of a very different sort on 3rd September 1916, when the first German Zeppelin destroyed during raids on this country was shot down in a field near the village by Lieutenant Leefe Robinson. When the news reached London large numbers of sightseers paid the shilling fare from King's Cross to Cuffley to visit the scene of the crash.

The extension north of Cuffley opened up more of the Hertfordshire countryside, and between the wars the area became very popular with ramblers. The LNER encouraged this traffic by issuing walking tour tickets available on the outward journey to one station and on the return from another. For 2s 3d, for example, one could travel from King's Cross to Cuffley, and return from Broxbourne to Liverpool Street; similarly a half crown ticket was available from Liverpool Street to Rye House, returning from Bayford to King's Cross. The company also published a guide to *Rambles in Hertfordshire* from places reached by its trains. One of the walks began and finished at Bayford:

> The pretty wooded countryside passed through on this walk is not at all well known to the rambler, and one may walk in it for miles even at weekends without meeting anyone . . . Bayford station, a few hundred yards from the village, is prettily situated amid fields, and forms an excellent jumping-off place for ramblers, as numbers of them are now beginning to realise.

In those days Bayford Station was lit by oil lamps and approached down an unmade road; even today it is still in a very rural situation.

North of Hertford, traffic never developed to any great extent. After the loop was completed a steam railcar service of five trains a day each way was put on between Hertford North and Stevenage, serving the intermediate stations at Stapleford and Watton-at-Stone. Some of the trains provided through services between Hertford North and Letchworth, Baldock or Royston via Stevenage and Hitchin. But no attempt was made to develop through traffic over the loop, and the existence of a parallel road between Hertford and Stevenage discouraged local traffic on the railway. Consequently the trains were withdrawn on the outbreak of the Second World War, and Stapleford and Watton Stations were closed after a life of only 15 years.

Competition

From time to time during the early years of the present century, the GNR's strong competitive position on the Enfield line was challenged by threats from other forms of transport. As early as 1902 a proposal was made for a tube railway from Hammersmith to Southgate via Piccadilly Circus, Cannon Street, Dalston, Tottenham and Palmers Green, with a throughout fare of twopence! Thanks to strong opposition from existing railways and local interests (including Lord Robert Cecil on behalf of Southgate cricket ground), the scheme was rejected. Conscious of the potential threat of any rival railway, however, the GNR secured in the same year restrictive covenants preventing any tube railway terminating at Finsbury Park from being extended northwards; these subsequently applied to the Great Northern & City Railway, opened from Moorgate Street in 1904, and the Great Northern, Piccadilly & Brompton Railway, opened from Hammersmith in

1906. By 1908 the idea of a tube railway in the Southgate area seemed so remote that the editor of a local newspaper declared:

There is not the slightest chance of such a line ever being constructed to Southgate . . . Such railways cost too much and do not pay . . . I fancy the originator of the story was someone who owned land in or near the village, and hoped to get a boom.

Meanwhile, the electric tramway was being extended along the Green Lanes from Wood Green, reaching Palmers Green in June 1907, Winchmore Hill in June 1908, and Enfield in July 1909, thus paralleling the GNR Enfield branch all the way. The trams, connecting with the newly opened tubes at Finsbury Park, provided new routes to the City and the West End, and encouraged residential development near the Green Lanes. Although much of their traffic came from areas less conveniently served by the railway, it is reported that the GNR suffered some loss of business, particularly at Palmers Green and Winchmore Hill. The railway company's policy of meeting the competition by raising fares did not win popular approval!

Despite this dubious commercial approach, the GNR was alive to the threat of competition, and by 1913 had prepared some ambitious plans for the Enfield branch. These consisted of:

1. Electrification to Finsbury Park to permit through running to Moorgate over the Great Northern & City Railway, with a subsequent connection to the Waterloo & City Railway at Bank.

2. Widening the line to four tracks between Bowes Park and Gordon Hill (some of the land acquired for this purpose may still be seen).

3. Construction of a new four platform station at Palmers Green.

4. Construction of a new railway (referred to as the Northern Junction), from Palmers Green to Brentford via Neasden, where a junction would be made with the Metropolitan Railway to form a new Outer Circle.

The electrification scheme was seen as an attempt to counter bus and tramway competition, and in its proposal to run trains to Moorgate over the GN & CR was the forerunner of the scheme which is now being implemented some 60 years later. The enlarged station at Palmers Green was required to cater for the expected increase in traffic from the Hertford and Stevenage extension, and, judging from a report in October 1913, would have been an impressive affair:

In something like six months time a large body of workmen will be engaged in demolishing the present inadequate station, built in 1871 – when the needs of the district were modest indeed compared with its present growth – and constructing a building really worthy of the district . . . The present booking offices on the bridge leading to Alderman's Hill will disappear, and on a new approach road sweeping from Fox Lane to Alderman's Hill, at the back of Old Park Road, fine new station premises will be erected, equipped with every modern convenience.

The writer could scarcely have foreseen that the original station of 1871 would still be in use some 60 years later!

Not surprisingly, the most controversial of these proposals was the construction of the Northern Junction Railway, referred to by its critics as 'the serpent in the garden'. From the junction at Palmers Green this would have skirted Broomfield Avenue, and would then have crossed Pymmes Brook and Powys Lane on an arch 44 ft high. After crossing Bowes Road the line would have roughly followed the route of the present day North Circular Road on its way to Brentford. It is not difficult to imagine the effect this would have had on Palmers Green as a residential area, and in the opening months of 1914 there was much verbal and written opposition to the scheme. The following is typical of the opinions expressed:

> Apart from the ugly embankment, which will spoil the appearance of the district to everyone coming along the line to Palmers Green with the idea of taking a house there, the projected goods siding would spell disaster. If anyone doubts the effect of goods shunting at night, one should make inquiries in that part of Stapleton Hall Road which runs from Harringay Station down as far as the Midland line . . . Besides these inconveniences which would destroy all the advantages which that part of Palmers Green possesses as a residential area, the outlook from the public park would be ruined; in fact, the whole area would be given over to noise and ugliness.

Fortunately for Palmers Green, the preservationists won the day, and the Railway Bill was stopped. But not only was the Northern Junction Railway abortive; the outbreak of the First World War effectively put a stop to the electrification of the Enfield branch and the reconstruction of Palmers Green Station.

By the end of the First World War, suburban growth along the Green Lanes, and increasing congestion at the Finsbury Park tram and tube interchange, had led to further demands for transport improvements north of this point. In 1919 local MPs took up the case for a tube railway from Finsbury Park to Hertford, but the restrictive covenants of 1902 prevented anything being done. Shortly after its formation in 1923, however, the LNER looked again at the electrification proposals for the King's Cross suburban lines, and undertook either to carry these out or to waive the veto on tube construction. Unfortunately for the financially weak LNER, there was already an over provision of transport north of Finsbury Park, where suburban railway, tramcars, 'General' buses and 'pirate' buses were all competing for traffic. In this situation the LNER could not find any financial justification for its electrification scheme, and in 1925 decided not to go ahead with it. Consequently the way was opened for a tube extension.

In the same year, the North and North East London Traffic Enquiry reported on how the transport needs of the area might best be met, and criticised the LNER for not electrifying its suburban lines. In failing to do so the company had 'exhibited a want of consideration for the needs of suburban traffic which the travelling public . . . feel they are entitled to expect'. The result was a recommendation that the Piccadilly Line should be extended north of Finsbury Park. Although there was public pressure for a route parallel to the LNER line through Harringay to Palmers Green and Enfield, the route finally selected was midway between the Great Northern main line and the Hertford Loop, where there was greater potential for housing development. The extension reached Arnos Grove in September 1932, Enfield West (later Oakwood) in March 1933 and Cockfosters in July 1933.

It was claimed in defence of the Piccadilly extension that it would not compete strongly with the LNER suburban lines because it would serve the West End rather than the City. Nevertheless, the LNER firmly opposed the scheme, complaining of the new railway 'coming into our territory and taking our traffic'. These fears were indeed justified, the tube offering better sited stations, more frequent trains and cheaper fares (in 1933 the fare to King's Cross from Enfield Chase was 1s 2d, whereas from Enfield West it was only sevenpence). Consequently the LNER lost much traffic to the Piccadilly extension, particularly at those stations which were close to the new tube stations. Bowes Park, for example, formerly one of the busiest stations on the Great Northern suburban system, lost many of its passengers to Bounds Green tube station a few hundred yards down the road. Palmers Green, a safer distance from the new tube, remained busy, but ceased to be the station for Southgate. The tube also generated a large amount of new traffic as the speculative builder moved in, and in less than five years the small villages and open farmland between Arnos Grove and Cockfosters were transformed into a sprawling suburb.

Postwar Revival

In the years leading up to the Second World War the fortunes of the Hertford Loop deteriorated, and with the war came the inevitable cutbacks in service. The City services were the hardest hit, bomb damage causing their suspension in the early years of the war. The Broad Street services were not restored until 1945, the Moorgate services a year later. The Broad Street trains, which had been provided by the LMS Railway before the war, were taken over by the LNER afterwards, and for the first time ran beyond Cuffley. But the City services were never restored to their prewar level, and by 1952, four years after the line had become part of the Eastern Region of British Railways, only about a third of the 40 or so trains running in each direction on weekdays were to or from the City stations. At this time the Hertford North service was running at hourly intervals outside peak periods, and the journey from Hertford to King's Cross took about an hour. With an unattractive service and run down equipment the line continued to lose traffic in the early postwar period.

Then, in 1955, the British Railways Modernisation Plan was published. This provided, once again, for electrification of the King's Cross suburban lines, including the Hertford Loop. Completion was planned for the early 1960s, so as a temporary measure diesel traction was introduced, the first diesel trains appearing on the Hertford North line in 1959. These were to be more than the 'stop gap' originally intended, however, for the electrification plan was again shelved, and the diesel railcars, supplemented in peak hours by locomotive hauled trains of compartment stock, have continued in use. (The locomotive hauled carriages, their compartments decorated with watercolour scenes of places served by the LNER, are the last of their kind on British Rail.) The diesel trains succeeded in regaining some of the lost traffic, and by 1961 there were 54 weekday trains in each direction. By this time peak hour commuters were benefiting from faster journey times made possible by a new 'skip-stop' timetable, the off peak frequency had been improved to half hourly, and the journey time from Hertford North to King's Cross had been reduced to about 50 minutes.

Following withdrawal of the Hertford – Stevenage service in 1939, few regular passenger trains ran beyond Hertford North for some years. After the war, however, this section of line was used from time to time on summer Saturdays by holiday trains between branch stations and east coast resorts, such as the Enfield – Skegness service which operated for a period. These were supplemented on occasions by seasonal excursions, some of which also ran over the northern part of the loop. Among the places visited were King's Lynn, Hunstanton, Clacton and Southend (the last two via Finsbury Park and Stratford), and combined rail and road excursions were run from Palmers Green, Enfield Chase and Hertford North to the Lincolnshire Bulb Fields.

Regular passenger services north of Hertford were reintroduced in March 1962, when a new diesel service was started between Hertford North and Stevenage to cater for factory and office workers during the week and for shopping and recreational travel on Saturdays. Stapleford and Watton Stations were not however reopened. This service is still running, and now consists of a few peak period trains on weekdays between London and Stevenage or Hitchin via Hertford, and an approximately hourly service on Saturdays. Some of the trains provide connections at Stevenage with main line services, and one or two run through to or from Huntingdon and Peterborough. Apart from an initial burst of publicity when it was introduced, the service has not been widely advertised.

Local freight traffic on the Hertford Loop has always been subordinate to the passenger service, and all the local goods and coal depots have been closed. In 1962 a new coal concentration depot was opened at Enfield Chase to replace a number of smaller yards. It was situated at the approach to the old Enfield terminus on the branch line from Grange Park. This too has now been closed, and the branch line removed. The only freight terminal remaining on the loop today is the rail connected oil depot at Watton-at-Stone.

Some major civil engineering works have been undertaken on the Hertford Loop in recent years. In 1959 a big track improvement scheme was carried out between Wood Green and Hertford North, enabling the maximum speed to be raised from 50 to 70 miles an hour. While the work was in progress buses replaced the train service, and they were followed by vans carrying passengers' luggage and prams. In 1965 the original bridge carrying the railway over Bowes Road, between Bowes Park and Palmers Green, was replaced by a new steel bridge, enabling improvements to be undertaken on the North Circular Road. The new bridge was erected on temporary trestles alongside the old one, and rolled into position one weekend. Then in 1970 a new bridge was constructed over the railway between Palmers Green and Winchmore Hill to eliminate a dangerous road junction where Hoppers Road meets Bourne Hill. This bridge consists of a 100 ft span of reinforced concrete beams spanning a gap of only 33 ft, and was said at the time to be the most heavily 'skewed' bridge of its type. The delicate operation of positioning the beams was carried out one Sunday. Also in 1970, a major resignalling scheme was authorised for the King's Cross suburban lines, including the Hertford Loop. This involves the installation of modern colour light signalling, and replacement of the old manual signalboxes and semaphore signals. Under this scheme the Hertford Loop will be controlled from a new signalling centre at King's Cross.

Then in 1971, the line's centenary year, the long awaited electrification scheme, proposed and shelved on several occasions since it was first suggested early this century, was at last authorised. This multi-million pound scheme covers all the

King's Cross suburban services as far out as Royston. Work on the Welwyn Garden City and Hertford North lines should be completed during 1976. This will entail the diversion of all Hertford North trains to Moorgate via Finsbury Park and the Northern City Line, which has been transferred from London Transport to British Rail. For West End passengers, cross-platform interchange with the Victoria Line will be provided at Highbury. This means that for the first time in its history, the Northern City Line (formerly the Great Northern & City Railway) will be used for the purpose for which it was originally built – as a City extension of the suburban lines. Diversion of the Hertford North services away from King's Cross and Broad Street will sever the century old direct link which the Enfield line has had with these terminals.

The Line Today

Over the first 3½ miles, from Wood Green to Grange Park, the passenger is following the original route of the Enfield branch line, laid down over a century ago.

Leaving Wood Green Station, five miles from King's Cross, the train immediately climbs a steep gradient onto a flyover which carries the Down Hertford line over the East Coast Main Line. On the left the main line can be seen entering the south end of Wood Green Tunnel, while on the right are the large carriage sheds at Bounds Green. The train then passes the connecting line to Palace Gates

Winchmore Hill Station, c. 1886. The station master is standing on the Up platform (left), nearest the camera. His house is on the extreme right.

before running under Bounds Green Road into Bowes Park Station, consisting of a single island platform.

Between Bowes Park and Palmers Green the line crosses the North Circular Road on the bridge rebuilt in 1965, and then runs on an embankment across the valley of Pymmes Brook, overlooking, on the right, a section of the New River. Before entering Palmers Green Station the train passes the former goods and coal yards, no longer rail connected, and beyond the goods yard, on the left, the station house.

Until recent alteration, Palmers Green Station retained much of its original appearance, and the twin gabled station building on the Aldermans Hill bridge had changed very little in over 100 years. Until a few years ago there was an iron footbridge connecting the former Fox Lane entrance on the Down platform with the Up platform. Platform extensions built some years ago in preparation for electrification are now out of use and overgrown.

Beyond Palmers Green the line runs in a cutting, spanned at one point by the new Bourne Hill bridge. The original bridge, now used only by pedestrians, follows immediately. After passing under the long skew bridge carrying Hoppers Road over the railway, the train enters Winchmore Hill Station. This was built on a similar pattern to Palmers Green, but the station building has now lost its west wing, which was demolished in 1965 because of subsidence. The signalbox, now removed, was in an unusual position under the stairs on the Up platform. The

Platform view of the old Enfield terminus before closure in 1910. The new high level station which replaced it later became Enfield Chase.

station house, also demolished, overlooked the platforms from the top of the cutting on the Down side.

After leaving Winchmore Hill the train passes on the left the site of the old goods yard, and then runs on an embankment and across Green Dragon Lane to Grange Park. It was on this section of the line that so much difficulty was experienced during construction. Grange Park Station, perched high on the embankment, is connected to the street level booking office by long sloping footpaths. From its Down platform there are extensive views across Enfield Golf Course to Trent Park.

Immediately beyond Grange Park the old line to Enfield diverged to the left to reach the original terminus, no longer rail connected. Although this has been closed to passengers for more than 60 years, substantial remains may still be seen, including the platform and the large station house with a frontage on Windmill Hill (most of the platform canopy and buildings were destroyed by fire a few years ago). In August 1961 the old station came briefly to life again when it was visited by a special steam hauled train for railway enthusiasts, which was making a tour of some of the lesser used lines in North and East London. This was possibly the first passenger train ever to travel from Euston to Enfield, the route being via Willesden Junction, Gospel Oak and Harringay.

From Grange Park, the newer line curves into Enfield Chase Station, nine miles from King's Cross. This is built on an embankment immediately to the south of Windmill Hill, and steps connect the platforms to the street level booking office and forecourt. After crossing Windmill Hill on an ornate girder bridge, the line continues on embankment towards Gordon Hill. It crosses Chase Green Avenue on a fine three arch brick bridge, which was required by Act of Parliament to be built to a high standard of appearance, apparently to satisfy local residents. Gordon Hill Station, the limit of the built up area, has four platforms, and a street level booking office in red brick very similar to the one at Grange Park. The old signal-box, at the south end of the station, is one of only two now surviving on the loop. At Hillyfields the line crosses the 14 arch Rendlesham Viaduct, approximately 70 ft high and nearly 500 ft long. Only two of its piers are built of solid brickwork; the remaining 11 are of concrete faced with brindled bricks. After skirting Crews Hill Golf Course, the line enters Crews Hill Station, in a semi-rural situation just south of the boundary between Enfield and Hertfordshire. Between here and Cuffley a tributary of Cuffley Brook is crossed on Soper's Farm Viaduct, approximately 55 ft high and consisting of 11 arches. Cuffley and Goff's Oak Station, though a modest affair similar to Crews Hill, serves a developing residential area.

North of Cuffley the train runs through undulating countryside, and shortly plunges into the darkness of Ponsbourne Tunnel, which carries the line under Ponsbourne Park. At 1 mile 926 yards, this was the longest tunnel on the GNR. Its other claim to fame is that during the last war it was used on occasions as an overnight refuge for the royal train when the King and other members of the Royal Family were making journeys from the North and bombing raids were taking place on London. The story was revealed in the London *Evening News* a few months after the war ended:

> Whenever the Royal Train was returning to London from the North of England and was due for a night in the tunnel, a code word would be flashed from one signal box to another, the line would be cleared, and the train service suspended for as long as necessary . . .

While the train was there soldiers guarded the wooded approaches to the tunnel, and two engines were held in readiness so that the train could be drawn out of the tunnel in either direction in the event of one end being blocked.

It was reported that on one occasion Winston Churchill was aboard the train when it spent a night in the tunnel.

Daylight suddenly appears as the line curves towards the north end of the tunnel, and the train emerges into a short cutting before arriving at Bayford, a simple country station surrounded by fields at the far end of the village. Beyond Bayford the line continues through open countryside, and then passes through a cutting below Bayfordbury Park before reaching the outskirts of Hertford. The River Lee is crossed on the 50 ft high Horn's Mill Viaduct, which is shortly followed by Hertford Viaduct, over the River Mimram. Beneath one span of this viaduct ran the old line from Welwyn; the track has now been removed, but its course can still be seen down in the valley on the left. Then on the right hand side comes the old Hertford North signalbox, which has been retained under the resignalling scheme.

Hertford North Station, 19½ miles from King's Cross and at the western edge of the town, was built with four platforms. The easternmost one has never been used, however – a reminder of the unrealised hopes which the railway had for the growth of the town. From the east side of the station the old line from Welwyn to the original GNR terminus in Hertford curved away on an embankment (sections of which are still visible), to join the former Great Eastern branch from Broxbourne at Hertford East.

The train leaves Hertford North on an embankment, then enters Molewood Tunnel, 365 yards long and built on a curve. Beyond the tunnel the line passes above the village of Waterford, and follows the valley of the River Beane through sandpit workings and farmland to Stapleford, which lies down below the railway on the right. The site of Stapleford Station can still be seen. Beyond Stapleford the line continues mostly in cutting to Watton-at-Stone, also situated to the right of the railway. The site of Watton Station can also be seen. Both Watton and Stapleford were simple country stations without booking offices. On the right past Watton Station is a small rail connected oil terminal. Beyond Watton a long straight stretch of line brings the train to the outskirts of Stevenage, where the Down line diverges from the Up to pass under the East Coast Main Line, which it joins at Langley Junction. From there the Hertford trains follow the main line to Stevenage and Hitchin, where most of them terminate.

ONE MONDAY evening in mid-August, some 15 years ago, an unexpected comedy was enacted on the Hertford Loop, when the sober routine of the railway was interrupted by an incident reported the following day in the *Daily Telegraph:*

> **Guard chases train**
>
> A railway guard chased his train for about a mile between Bowes Park and Palmers Green stations on the Eastern Region last night. When, out of breath, he came in sight of Palmers Green, he saw the train pull out again, with a local porter acting as guard.

The guard had waved his green flag for the 5.5 pm from Broad Street to Gordon Hill to leave Bowes Park, when he saw a child board a London-bound train and leave the carriage door open. He ran across the platform to shut it, only to find that his own train had departed, and with commendable devotion to duty decided to give chase. His feelings on reaching Palmers Green will have been shared by many a tardy commuter!

Bibliography

The development of the railway:

G. H. Lake and R. A. H. Weight: *The Wood Green-Langley Junction Line of the Eastern Region* (Railway Pictorial and Locomotive Review, Aug/Sept and Oct/Nov 1949).

J. N. Young: *100 Years of the Enfield Branch* (Railway World, April 1971).

C. H. Grinling: *The History of the Great Northern Railway* (first published 1898, new edition with additional chapters 1966).

H. P. White: *A Regional History of the Railways of Great Britain. Volume 3, Greater London* (1963).

D. I. Gordon: *A Regional History of the Railways of Great Britain. Volume 5, Eastern Counties* (1968).

Railway official timetables and handbills.

Various articles in the *Railway Magazine.*

Competitive transport:

T. A. Gibbs: *The Metropolitan Electric Tramways. A Short History* (1962).

A. A. Jackson and D. F. Croome: *Rails Through the Clay. A History of London's Tube Railways* (1962).

The railway in its local setting:

J. Thorne: *Handbook to the Environs of London* (1876).

Miss H. Cresswell: *Winchmore Hill. Memories of a Lost Village* (1912).

H. G. Regnart: *Memories of Winchmore Hill* (1952).

T. Mason: *A Southgate Scrap-Book* (1948).

H. W. Newby: *'Old' Southgate* (1949).

C. W. Whitaker: *An Illustrated Historical, Statistical and Topographical Account of the Urban District of Enfield* (1911).

Industrial Archaeology in Enfield (Enfield Archaeological Society, 1971).

Where to Live Round London (Northern Side) (The Homeland Association, 1906).

Rambles in Hertfordshire (LNER, c.1935).

Local newspapers:
Enfield Observer
Enfield Gazette and Observer
Recorder for Palmers Green, Winchmore Hill and Southgate
Palmers Green and Southgate Gazette

90p

42

A Guide to......
Cockatiels
and their Mutations

Their Management, Care & Breeding

By Peggy Cross and Diana Andersen

Published and Edited by Australian Birdkeeper ©

First Published 1994 by
Australian Birdkeeper
PO Box 6288,
South Tweed Heads,
NSW. 2486. Australia.
Reprinted 1996.

ISBN 0 9587455 8 7

Front Cover:
Top left: Yellowface cock
Centre left: Whiteface split Pied cock
Bottom left: Pair of Normal Cockatiels
Bottom right: Heavily marked Pied hen
Back Cover: Normal Cockatiel cock

All photographs by Diana Andersen

PROUDLY PUBLISHED & PRINTED IN AUSTRALIA

Design, Type and Art: PrintHouse Multimedia Graphics (Gold Coast)
Colour Separations: Oceangraphics (Gold Coast)
Printing: HBM Print (Brisbane)

About the Authors

Peggy Cross

Peggy arrived in Perth, Western Australia on 23 December 1978 with firm plans to return to Seattle, Washington in eight months. The Boeing contract for the Northwest Shelf Oil Project was extended many times and this family are now Australian citizens. The amusement of a few budgies started the study of aviculture. A grey cockatiel hen was obtained as a pet. This 'pet' project failed and she was intrigued to learn that a 'white' bird paired with the hen would produce ... what was that again? This was quickly followed by WHY?, and that question still keeps her hobby interesting.

A proud and loyal founding member of the Aviary Bird Association in WA, Peggy is currently a committee member of the Avicultural Society of Southern Tasmania. For many years she has contributed avicultural articles to various organisations, including Australian Birdkeeper. Particularly enjoyable has been the opportunity to visit avicultural clubs in other states to speak about her interest in birds. She was invited to speak on cockatiels at the AFA Convention in Melbourne 1994.

While in WA Peggy kept and bred many of the Australian cockatoos and a wide variety of other Australian parrots. With the move to Tasmania the collection was reduced considerably. Now that aviaries are established, a wider variety of special birds are acclimatising happily. The Major Mitchell cockatoos and Red and White-tailed Black cockatoos are thriving, also psephotus, neophemas and a variety of rosellas. Many of the choices also reflect her interest in mutations.

Tasmania offers a wonderful environment, similar to the northwest of the United States, and the family lives only 20 minutes from Hobart, in a rural setting. With the distinct change of seasons birds have the stimulation of natural breeding cycles. The Doberman family transplanted happily and thoroughly enjoy their duties in the aviary areas where they are suitably territorial, and compete with the cockatoos for the odd chop bone or almond.

An added bonus is the enjoyment of a wide variety of native animals such as the ubiquitous possums, barred bandicoot, Eastern quoll (which at first was mistaken for a feral cat), echidna, long-nosed potoroo, Tasmanian bettong, pademelon, wallabies, and the odd grey kangaroo. To her relief, Tasmanian Devils apparently do not live in the area.

The surrounding trees host Tasmanian green rosellas (*Platycercus caledonicus*), the local eastern rosella (*Platycercus eximus dimenensis*) and yellow tailed black cockatoos as well as a huge variety of local softbills. Wedgetail eagles nest on the hill above and as many as seven sometimes soar overhead together.

Diana Andersen

Diana is one of the few people who have actually researched their bird interest before obtaining birds.

She has been an active member of the Aviary Bird Association in Western Australia, where she is currently Secretary, and regularly contributes thoughtful articles about cockatiels and their management to various organisations. Her thorough, progressive attitude has contributed much to the advancement of the quality cockatiels that we now assume will be the standard of birds we enjoy. A jewellery maker by trade, she approaches the care and breeding of cockatiels as a different sort of artistic production, and the beautiful birds that result reflect that care.

Her bird collection now includes a careful selection of cockatoos, psephotus parrots, polytelis parrots and others in a rainbow of colours for added interest. With the increase in quantity and variety she also has obtained and trained to champion status a pair of energetic cattle dogs. These interesting dogs provide an enthusiastic early warning, search and destroy capability to (and for) her varied family.

Situated in the hills above Perth, Western Australia, Diana is frequently visited by wild flocks of galahs, twenty-eights, Western rosellas and Red-capped parrots and occasionally, Purple-crowned lorikeets, and Red and White-tailed Black cockatoos.

Contents

Left: Whiteface Pearl hen.
Above: Yellowface pair.
Below: Normal cock, Whiteface Cinnamon hen and Lutino Cinnamon Pearl Pied hen.

Introduction

The beloved cockatiel, now recognised as the smallest member of the cockatoo family, is one of the most popular aviary or pet birds in the world.

Cockatiels are the perfect bird, suiting all types of interests and needs. Their charming personality, eagerness to breed and hardy constitution keep them in constant demand.

Cockatiels will learn to mimic human sounds, can learn to whistle opera arias with enthusiasm, sound like a telephone (and also call their human friend to answer it), bark like the resident dog or mimic any bird that happens to live near it for a length of time. They will quickly learn to imitate the microwave beep or any other sound repeatedly heard in your home if housed indoors.

They will cheerfully include you in their family and allow you to participate in the planning and raising of their young, sometimes to your embarrassment. If you need a loyal friend or a constant companion a cockatiel can make you the centre of its life. That is quite a responsibility and before adopting a young bird for a pet you should consider carefully if you can live up to your pet's needs.

For those beginning in aviculture and wanting to enjoy a hardy, undemanding bird in a back yard aviary, again, the cockatiel is an ideal subject. Reasonable housing and a sensible, varied diet will see your cockatiels live long and productive lives.

Breeders who want to learn, develop or improve a strain of birds will find the cockatiel an ideal bird. With a long list of already recognised mutations and more being added, a lifetime could be spent developing this facet of cockatiel husbandry.

History

Cockatiels have been described in literature since the 1700's. They were displayed at the *Jardin des Plantes*, Paris 1846, and were bred successfully there. The cockatiel was considered an established aviary bird in Europe by 1884 and was established in the United States by 1910. Cockatiels have been bred in Australia since 1901. Interest in this underrated bird accelerated when the lutino mutation appeared in 1958.

The name cockatiel is generally accepted to be an adaptation of a Dutch/Portuguese word that, translated, means little cockatoo. Much has been written discussing and changing scientific names for this bird. I am content to use *Nymphicus hollandicus (Kerr).*

The cockatiel now comes in many variations of colour and pattern but the original grey bird should be used as a baseline for size and stature. Domestic diets and controlled breeding have provided the atmosphere for the cockatiel to increase in size, a development no doubt encouraged by market demands, but one which needs to be closely monitored to retain the integrity of the wild type cockatiel.

Standards should be documented in an attempt to keep the perfect and ideal cockatiel just that, not bigger, longer, fluffy or whatever. Every effort should be made to ensure that our perfect normal cockatiel does not succumb to a fate similar to that of the now, almost unrecognisable show budgie.

Cockatiels are a small to medium sized parrot and should measure 300-330mm (12-13+ inches) in length. Some show standards encourage a larger bird, up to 350mm (14 inches). These measurements include their tapered, movable crest of 50mm or more (2-3 inches) and long, slender tail, which accounts for half their entire length. Normal weight is 90 to 120 grams (3 to 4 ounces).

The opening description from the Australian National Cockatiel Society Show Standard is succinct and ideal:

The cockatiel is a sleek bird with straight back and full chest, giving an overall look of a strong bird able to cover vast areas in its daily search for food.

Cockatiels cannot be dismissed as a 'grey bird'. Close observation will see shades of dove grey to charcoal throughout the normal bird's body. Tones of brown and an underlying yellow suffusion add to the depth of colour. All normal cockatiels have a pattern of white on their shoulders and flight feathers. This pattern fits together to form a white wing bar that is brightly visible at rest or in flight. When birds have a heavy yellow suffusion, this wing bar is streaked with yellow.

Mature cocks develop a bright yellow face and neck and feature an orange cheek patch. The yellow and orange in each bird varies in depth of colour and area covered. Adult cocks have dark grey under tail feathers. If a cock has some barred tail feathers, it is an indication of his youth. Their chests are uniformly grey. Cock birds have an upswept, movable crest that is coloured bright yellow from the face to about half its length, then it shades into grey tips. Their expressive crest is used for communication.

Hens have a similar amount of yellow and orange on their faces but the colour is overlaid with a suffusion of grey. Their under tail feathers are barred with yellow tones and they often have shaded grey or speckled chests. The crests on hens are primarily grey but are as expressive and long as the cock bird's.

When newly hatched, normal wild type cockatiels have yellow down and dark eyes. Juveniles have pinkish toned ceres which 'blush' when they are frightened or hurt. Young cockatiels appear darker in colour until powder down is produced in enough quantities that it can be dispersed throughout their feathers. This distribution softens cockatiel colours and also serves to make them waterproof.

Young cocks look much like hens until about four months of age when they begin to show yellow streaking on their faces and replace barred tail feathers with solid colour. Cockatiels have dark grey ceres, feet, toenails and dark brown eyes when adult.

Cockatiels are still known by regional colloquial names throughout Australia. Western Australians may refer to them as Weero or Weiro, names reportedly adapted from aboriginal words. Eastern Australian states commonly call them Quarrions.

The Naturalist's Library, consisting of 40 volumes dated 1833-1843, author William Jardine, features a hand painted Gould picture of the Red Cheeked Nymphious in Vol. 10. This bird was identified as *Nymphious Novae Hollandieae*. Observation clearly shows our native cockatiel. In other historical literature cockatiels have been known as Corella, Crested Parakeet, Crested Ground Parakeet, Grey Parrot, Yellow top-knotted Parrot, Cockatoo Parrot.

Cockatiels are distributed throughout Australia. However, most non-aviary sightings in Tasmania have probably been aviary escapees. Generally they avoid coastal areas unless the inland summers have been very dry. They then migrate closer to the coast where conditions are more favourable. Due to their ability to adapt they can be found anywhere in Australia where suitable food and water are available.

Observing cockatiels in the wild was a high priority for me whilst recently in the Northern Territory. Four hours south of Darwin at Pine Creek I sighted a small group of cockatiels. As I approached, the parents flew to a nearby dead tree. The hen remained clearly in sight but the cock bird positioned himself sideways along the branch and virtually disappeared from view. He and the branch were similar in colour. This made me realise that I may have travelled past many cockatiels without seeing them.

The seven youngsters remained at the side of the gravel road, busily pecking in one area. I continued to ease closer, taking photos, until they flew away and were joined by their parents. I spent some time trying to see what they were eating but never discovered anything I recognised. Either the seeds in this bare patch of fine gravel were too small for me to see or they were interested in the red, sandy gravel.

Perched on roadside telephone lines with their crests raised in alarm makes cockatiels in the wheat growing areas of Western Australia easily recognisable.

Acquiring Stock

Walk into any pet shop in Australia and you will find cockatiels offered for sale. These are usually normal greys and a few of the more common mutations such as lutino, pearl and pied.

For someone wanting a few cheerful, attractive birds for their backyard aviary, purchasing from a dealer or pet shop will probably suffice for their needs. However, for those interested in the breeding of colour mutations, it is best to acquire your birds from private breeders who close band their birds,

Above: Normal cock, Whiteface Cinnamon hen, Lutino Cinnamon Pearl Pied hen. Right: Normal hen and cock.

Normal hen & cock.

keep accurate records and can guarantee the genetic background of their birds.

For those wanting a pet, or a pair of pets as I would prefer to see them kept, the best birds to acquire are undoubtedly hand raised chicks. These are already accustomed to humans and used to being handled. The more gregarious individuals are immediately apparent, as they usually cling to the wire demanding human attention long after they have weaned.

Regardless of the purpose of the bird or birds you are acquiring, there are a few basic things to look for regarding the health and well being of the individuals you are selecting. One of the cockatiel's most endearing qualities is its active, happy disposition. When not sleeping, which it does through the middle of the day, it should be actively moving about, preening, feeding and investigating its area, making it relatively easy for the novice to choose a healthy bird.

If you are choosing birds in summer, go early in the morning before the heat has set in. At this time of day the birds should be active and an individual who appears sleepy and unwell will be more obvious. In very hot conditions, most cockatiels will rest on both feet with their wings held out, their feathers held close to their body and their beaks slightly open. This is definitely not their most flattering stance. Catching and transporting birds in heat is stressful and unwise.

In winter it is better to go late in the day when the birds begin their late afternoon feed. Again, at this time they should be active and not feeling the cold and therefore a bird that is still looking fluffed and dozing on two feet should be avoided.

The bird you choose should be a good size and in good feather relative to its age.

Cockatiels increase in size for at least twelve months. Even youngsters that have had severe health or injury setbacks will often reach normal size in this period with a good diet. Therefore I look for a bird that is a reasonable size for its age and I place much more emphasis on its conformation which will change to a lesser degree as the bird matures.

Young birds can look terribly small and scruffy when they go through their juvenile moult between four and six months of age. If you know for a fact that a bird you are hoping to purchase is this age then you can possibly excuse its appearance, however, it is probably best to choose only birds that are in good feather.

Adult cockatiels moult in January or February, though unusual weather patterns can often bring about early or late moults. Choosing a bird in perfect feather at this time of year can be difficult.

Extensive areas of missing feathers particularly around the back of the neck is often the result of over preening by other birds, particularly when the birds are being kept in overcrowded conditions with little to keep them occupied. This in itself, although unsightly, is harmless, though the perpetrator of the plucking will often turn into a plucking parent. On the other hand, any evidence of self mutilation or abnormal feathering should be avoided. Avoid birds missing feathers around the eyes as this can be a sign of a carrier of psittacosis, a highly contagious disease in birds. Also to be avoided are signs of heavy breathing, eye infections and nasal discharge, symptoms of the same disease and of ill health generally.

You should observe the birds closely for lameness and toe and beak abnormalities. Their vents and surrounding feathers should be clean and when the bird you have chosen is caught, you should feel a layer of firm muscle and flesh on either side of the keel bone. Sharp protruding keel bones are a sign of ill health or a serious worm problem.

For those people interested in competitively showing their birds, the Australian National Cockatiel Society can supply you with a copy of the Australian Show Standard. For those interested in simply breeding good quality birds, the show standard can be used as a guide. In time you will get a feel for quality birds and automatically know what to look for.

The most common mistake made is to breed for colour and markings with less emphasis on good conformation.

When purchasing birds sight unseen from breeders too distant to visit personally, you can only rely on the honesty of the breeder concerned when verbally representing their birds. All birds emerge from transport cages looking ruffled and stressed. Unless the birds are obviously poor or not at all what you wanted, final judgement on your new purchases should be reserved for at least a few days, preferably weeks, to allow the birds to settle in and regroom themselves. However, under no circumstances should you accept birds that you feel were misrepresented.

All new stock, regardless of species, should be quarantined for a period of at least four weeks, preferably six weeks, before being introduced to your other birds. During this time, your new birds should be treated for internal and external parasites to avoid introducing parasites to your existing birds, and should be closely observed for symptoms of illness.

Housing

One of the most common adjectives used to describe the cockatiel is 'hardy'. This term often translates to poor housing conditions in the belief that cockatiels are undemanding birds that will maintain good health and reproduce happily in anything from a wired-in fruit box in the backyard shed to a nest box in the corner of someone's lounge room!

While it is true that these tough little birds will endeavour to raise their young under all kinds of adverse conditions, supplying them with adequate housing is the minimum responsibility of all bird keepers. Supplying them with ideal housing will result in happier, healthier birds and in turn, they will reward their keepers with greater productivity.

There are three main methods of housing cockatiels - conventional aviaries, suspended aviaries and pet cages. There are several essential requirements that are common to all three.

These are: Protection from inclement weather, excessive heat and draught
Protection from vermin and predators
Access to sunlight for Vitamin D3
Escape proof safety areas
Easy access to fresh food and water
Adequate exercise area
Privacy

Conventional Aviaries

Whether it is an individual backyard aviary housing a mixed collection or a bank of breeding aviaries, an aviary is probably the most common form of housing for cockatiels.

Birds that are not paired and set up for breeding are frequently housed as same sex groups in large aviaries with long flight areas to encourage exercise. Aviaries should be at least 1.2 to 1.5 metres (4-5 feet) wide, a comfortable height to walk in and 2.4 metres (8 feet) long, preferably longer, as cockatiels will often revert to climbing from one end of the aviary to the other if the flights are too short. Lack of adequate exercise will result in overweight birds that can develop breeding problems. However, aviaries that are too long can occasionally result in fatalities in young birds who gain too much speed without enough control when leaving the nest.

We prefer fully covered flights to protect the birds from predators such as raptors, owls and cats and this also prevents droppings from wild birds entering the flights. A dim night light will virtually eliminate deaths, injuries and abandoned young due to night frights caused by predators and vermin.

A safety passage is highly recommended to prevent escapes and for extra protection from predators and if it is wide enough, allows

Above left: Suspended aviaries with the tarpaulin rolled back. Above right: Aviaries with the cover rolled down to protect from inclement weather and night frights. Right: Rear view of a row of suspendeds showing feeding verandah.

you to access the aviaries with a wheel barrow for cleaning. Cockatiels are notorious for shooting out of the aviary over the shoulder of the keeper. Numerous notices for cockatiels in the 'Lost and Found' section of the newspaper are testimony to this. Many breeders use the safety passage on their aviaries to exercise their birds. The birds generally return to their own aviary when someone approaches and the door can be simply closed behind them.

Many people like dirt floors so that the birds can forage on the ground, as they do in the wild. However, for health reasons, concrete floors are much safer. The birds are better off being supplied with a good quality mineral grit that meets any digestive requirements and has a much higher nutritional value than common garden sand. Vermin are much easier to control with concrete floors than with dirt floors and, with the correct slope on your aviary floors, droppings and other debris can be frequently hosed away reducing the likelihood of worm infestation.

Conventional aviaries must be designed to suit the climatic conditions where individual aviculturists live and manage their birds. Most areas of Australia require aviaries to face north, if at all possible, to gain maximum access to winter sunlight. Shelter should be provided at the back and at least a third of each side. This provides the birds with protection from the weather. Cockatiels are far more susceptible to draft than very cold conditions. Originally a desert bird, the cockatiel tolerates heat and cold quite well. The sheltered area provides them with some security and also privacy. Nest boxes hung in the sheltered area are usually accepted much more readily than those hung in the open.

A double roof is also recommended for people living in very hot climates, especially if you intend to encourage your birds to breed. This reduces the heat radiation into the aviaries considerably and temperatures remain more stable than with a sprinkler system on the roof, going on and off at regular intervals. Sprinkler systems are often used successfully, especially for the enjoyment of birds who prefer bathing in rain drops to happily splashing all the water out of a water dish. If sprinklers are combined with only a slight breeze the cooling effect is multiplied and, even in summer conditions, wind chill can affect young cockatiels who do not yet have the waterproofing protection of their powder down.

Wire feeding verandahs can be attached to conventional aviaries in the walkway, allowing for easy access to food and water dishes. These verandahs make it possible to service the needs of your birds without

Above: All wire suspended – suitable for pet cockatiels. Right: inside greenhouse showing metal flaps and nestboxes.

entering their aviary, except to clean and check the nest boxes. I believe that breeding birds who are not tame become much more settled in their environment if they are left in peace.

Suspended Aviaries

Suspended aviaries are used extensively by the authors as they are well suited to breeding cockatiels. One of the major criticisms of suspended cages or aviaries is that they are too small, causing feather disorders and overweight birds. The simple solution to this criticism is to make them the same length as conventional aviaries.

The suspended aviaries I have in Western Australia are 2.0 metres (7 feet) long with one third of the cage covered on the sides and top. This assists in creating a draft free environment for the birds. The nest boxes are mounted on the outside of the suspended, in the top left-hand corner. Most pairs readily accept the boxes in this position and the external access, with the inspection hatch at the back or side, makes monitoring of the eggs and chicks simple. The suspended breeding aviaries in Tasmania are housed in a large shed without individual covering for the cages. Nest boxes are positioned similarly and are accepted readily.

Another advantage of suspended aviaries is that the birds feel secure and become very settled. Their environment is not constantly being invaded by a large foreign body, often armed with a rake or broom. The worst that enters our aviaries is an occasional net. Even very nervous birds will perch close to the front of the aviary while I am standing close to it, making close observation of the birds easy. Suspendeds can be narrower than conventional aviaries without disadvantaging their flying space. Cockatiels can be colony bred but for accurate and controlled breeding results one pair per aviary is essential. My suspended aviaries for breeding are 2.0 metres (7 feet) long, 900mm (3 feet) wide and 1200mm (4 feet) high. This allows for a greater number of aviaries to be housed in a smaller area.

Suspendeds can be built as multiple divided units but this makes internal cleaning a little difficult. I prefer the cages to be built in individual units so they can be easily moved about or lifted down for cleaning. The frames of my aviaries are made from 20mm (${}^{3}/_{4}$inch) galvanised square tube with a large door fitted at one end. This enables me to enter the aviary when it is on the ground to replace the perches and scrub the wire when necessary. Individual suspended aviaries also have the added advantage of acting as double wiring with no more cost than building a row of conventional aviaries because of the wire saved by not building down to the ground.

Suspended aviaries are much easier to protect from mice and rats and it is easier to place baits in an aviary complex without risk to the birds. However, it is best to house suspendeds at least partially within another structure. This is to protect nest boxes and feed stations from the weather, provide security from predators and again to provide a safety area for handling the birds. If your structure is secure, there is the added advantage of being able to release tame birds into the area for added exercise and for the pleasure of handling your tame birds.

Feeding verandahs are fitted to the door of my suspended aviaries at about waist height and the nest boxes rest on top of these.

Hygiene is one of the greatest advantages of suspendeds, with most droppings, seed husks and vegetable bits falling through the wire. If larger pieces of uneaten food are removed daily and aviaries hosed down once a week, there is little risk of bacterial or fungal infections resulting from poor hygiene. The debilitating cycle of worm infestation will be broken as droppings will fall through the wire cage bottom.

Feed

Although seed will never be replaced as an integral part of the diet for most species of parrot, it should be considered the 'rice and potatoes' of your birds' diet, as it supplies many of the starches and carbohydrates our birds need. Even with a wide variety of green food, sprouts, vegetables and fruits many of the additional requirements of vitamins and minerals must be supplied in the form of dietary supplements.

Seed

We recommend and use a high quality small seed mix such as that sold to budgie breeders in preference to a small parrot mix for pet cockatiels. Quality budgie mix usually contains plain canary seed, various millets and a proportion of hulled oats. There are many larger seeds in some small parrot mixes which are unsuitable for cockatiels, resulting in considerable waste. Most cockatiels prefer to eat the smaller canary and millet seeds. Approximately 10% grey sunflower can be added, if desired, to a quality budgie mix.

As breeders, we prefer to mix our own seed so it remains consistent throughout the year. Our recipe is 25% plain canary, 25% Jap millet, 25% white millet and 25% hulled oats. The same mix is used in Tasmania and Western Australia. Some sunflower is added in Tasmania during winter and for breeding pairs. This basic dry seed mix is offered in hoppers at all times. It is important to try to obtain good quality, clean seed from a reliable source. If you are in doubt, the quality and freshness of your seed can be tested by soaking and sprouting. If seed is still viable, 95% should sprout within a few days. Seed that will not germinate is of no nutritional value.

In addition to dry seed, sprouted seed is offered on alternate days to all birds and every day to those that have been set up for breeding. To those birds with young in the nest, sprouted seed is supplied in virtually unlimited quantities. We find it is by far the best food for rearing chicks, being nutritious, bulky and easily digested. We use a mix of one part grey sunflower, one part whole wheat and one part whole oats (horse feed oats), with one half part of milo, a variety of sorghum.

Sunflower, wheat and milo sprout on the same time schedule in Tasmania, whereas whole oats take longer and must be sprouted separately.

Milo is the little round orange seed that I have never seen any type of bird eat when it appears in a seed mix. It is an inexpensive seed but, according to my seed charts, has similar nutrition to that of canary seed and millet. I've offered sprouted milo to my birds for more than one year now and only the 'Men Pen' still leave orange seeds on their plate. The 'Hen Pen' and all the youngsters in the 'Play Pen' choose sprouted milo as often as they choose sprouted wheat or sunflower.

Other suitable sprouting seeds are lupin, which is extremely high in protein; mung beans and pigeon peas. Individual plates of sprouts are sprinkled with a multivitamin prior to feeding and all uneaten sprouts are removed by the end of the day. Sprouts are served on clean plates each day and supplied to feeding parents as early in the morning as possible.

Sprouting needs to be done with care or the resulting fungal and bacterial growths within the mix can prove fatal to your birds. I strongly recommend the use of an

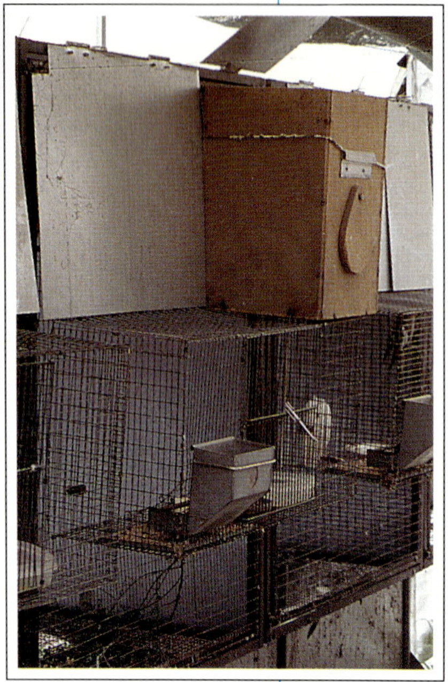

Above left: Feeding verandah fitted with an external nestbox.
Above right: Revolving feeders fitted to a feeding verandah.
Right: Feeding verandah.

antifungal, antibacterial agent throughout the sprouting process.

The procedure I use is as follows:

1. Place the seed mix into a plastic mesh colander and rinse until the water runs clean.
2. Empty the rinsed seed into a glass or stainless steel bowl and cover with a solution containing an antibacterial solution. I use Vetafarm 'Aviclens' .
3. After twelve to twenty-four hours, tip the seed back into the colander and rinse again. I rinse by placing the colander into a larger bowl, allowing rapidly running water to lift and separate the seed until the water runs clean.
4. Dunk the colander into a solution containing the antibacterial agent for ten minutes, then lift and drain.

5. Repeat the rinsing procedure followed by step 4 each day until the sprouts are ready to be fed. This will vary depending on the time of year, due to temperature changes. If you are using 'Aviclens' the sprouts can be fed after the final dip into the solution. If you are using some other form of antibacterial agent such as bleach you may need to rinse the solution off

Above: Minerals - cuttlefish, calcium and iodine bell mineral block. Murphy's™ Pro-system minerals, mixed grits and crushed shellgrit.
Below: Native food supplements. Eucalypt, acacia, lucerne tree, wild oats, veldt grass.

before feeding. It may sound as if I make up gallons of 'Aviclens' each day but this is not the case. I always start by rinsing the sprouts that are ready to be fed first, retaining the antibacterial solution for the subsequent batches of seed to be dipped into.

Greens

The more fruit and vegetables you can convince your pets or breeding birds to eat the better it is for their health. A common complaint is that the birds will not eat what is offered. Educating your birds to enjoy a healthy variety of food is a continuing process, but persistence pays off in the long run as birds that eat well tend to feed their chicks well. Young birds that have been fed a varied diet by their parents automatically eat a wide variety of foods.

The quickest way of educating your birds to eat new food is to place birds that are unaccustomed to eating a varied diet with young birds that eat everything that is offered. If you only have one or two pet cockatiels, introduce only one new type of food at a time, placing a fresh piece in their cage each day. Eventually the birds become accustomed to it in their personal area and they will nibble at it. In doing so, they discover that this new object is edible. It also helps to anchor the vegetable down with a cuttlefish clip.

Corn on the cob is particularly appreciated by feeding parents and is high in Vitamin A, a vitamin that is totally lacking in all seed diets. Celery, parsley, pumpkin, carrots, beans and apples are all suitable. I feed silverbeet on a daily basis, along with a choice of other vegetables as available. I blanch silverbeet for ten seconds in boiling water to break down the oxalic acid it contains and remove any pesticides. I do so because the oxalic acid prevents some absorption of calcium. I find that parents readily feed the softened silverbeet to newly hatched chicks. It is obviously very nutritious and easily digested. All uneaten greens must be removed at the end of the day to prevent the birds eating greens that have begun to go mouldy.

Native Foods

Eucalyptus, with or without buds and flowers, Wattle, Casuarinas, Bottlebrush, Melaleucas and Lucerne tree (a cattle fodder tree) are all enjoyed and recommended for cockatiels. There may be some benefits to feather lustre from feeding Eucalypts because of the oils contained in their leaves. The most obvious benefit of feeding native bushes is stress reduction. Branches will occupy the chewing desires of cockatiels for hours, resulting in a lower incidence of behavioural disorders such as excessive preening, both of themselves and other aviary occupants. This is particularly important for pet cockatiels that have little to occupy them in their confined cages.

Seeding Grasses

Seeding heads are particularly appreciated by all my birds, especially feeding parents. Wild oats, veldt grass and feed oats are readily taken, even by birds unaccustomed to a varied diet. If these are unavailable in your area you can sow garden pots with the seed you are currently feeding. When your crop reaches the point where seeding heads are about to open and drop their seeds, it's time to cut the sprays and feed them to your birds. They will attack the seeding heads with obvious pleasure. Lucerne, or alfalfa, is a highly nutritious, easy to grow perennial green food.

Bread

We feed multi-grain bread on a daily basis. An aviary containing ten birds receives one slice. Parents feeding four or five chicks in the nest would receive a full slice first thing in the morning and up to a full slice again late in the afternoon. Don't give them an unlimited supply, as some parents have been known to raise their chicks entirely on bread, resulting in nutritional disorders.

Vitamins

It is impossible to guarantee that your birds are eating everything that you offer. To compensate for any dietary deficiencies, I use a multivitamin powder. There are several available specifically formulated for birds. These are formulated to dissolve in the drinking water or be sprinkled over greens. Multivitamins in the water can promote the growth of bacteria and even though I change the water daily, I prefer to use it as a sprinkle. I use a large commercial salt shaker to sprinkle the powder over my sprouted seed. Excessive use of multivitamins can cause problems, so the manufacturer's directions should be followed. One of the major benefits of using a vitamin supplement is that when there are a large number of chicks in the nest the smallest chicks will receive the essential nutrients required for normal growth, even if they are achieving a smaller volume of food.

Minerals and Grit

This is one of the most neglected areas of feeding. Birds require soluble and insoluble grit in their diet. Insoluble grit aids in digestion by grinding up seed in the crop and is particularly important for birds kept in pet cages or suspended cages without access to sand and dirt floors. Soluble grit is the major source of minerals in a bird's diet and is essential for the well being and successful breeding of all birds.

My birds are supplied with a mixture of crushed shell grit and two types of mixed grit - one containing a red gravel and one containing charcoal. Any form of calcium that is readily taken by laying hens is worthwhile including in your birds' diet. We use a mineral supplement called 'Murphy's Pro-System' minerals sold by 'Golden Cob'. It contains calcium, biotin and iodine and is eaten enthusiastically by breeding hens. Since using it I have had consistently high fertility rates and a reduced incidence of feather plucking in the nest. Biotin is often used to treat feather disorders, perhaps plucking and feather disorders are linked in some way.

Our birds have access to cuttlefish, calcium and iodine bells and mineral blocks such as those used for cattle. The bells and blocks are there to help keep beaks and nails trim, as well as supplying minerals. Iodine blocks placed in the nest might help reduce plucking. I am not sure if this suggests that plucking parents are in need of iodine or whether the blocks simply occupy the parents while they are in the nest, thus distracting them from plucking their chicks as a form of amusement. The use of 1 teaspoon iodised salt to 1 litre of water as drinking water is recommended by some veterinarians as a help for feather plucking. Lack of salt or iodine may predispose some birds to pluck.

Protein

Cockatiels often enjoy small amounts of cheese, crushed unsalted nuts and hard-boiled egg. I sometimes use a mixture of these to supply protein. Remove any leftover mix from the aviaries before it becomes rancid.

Water

Dirty water is one of the primary causes of illness and death in aviary birds. I prefer to use glazed or stainless steel non-porous dishes. I provide fresh water daily and use 'Aviclens' in my water dishes to prevent bacterial growth. The dishes are removed once a week and replaced with clean dishes. This may seem like over protection but even after the daily measures I use, the water dishes that are collected at the end of the week have a sour odour. While adult birds may tolerate a certain level of bacteria, young chicks are more vulnerable.

Breeding/Sexing

While there are many factors that govern the successful breeding of any species, one thing remains common to all - the need for a cock and a hen. This may seem a simple thing to determine when discussing cockatiels, normally a sexually dimorphic species, but it is always surprising how many people get it wrong. The confusion appears to arise because mutation factors alter the accepted visual sex characteristics in both colour and feather pattern. For instance, the cinnamon and fallow mutations allow hens to display considerably more yellow on their faces than normal hens. They do not, however, have anywhere near the amount of yellow that a cock bird develops nor does a hen of this mutation have the same clearly defined edge of the facial mask that the cock does. Lutino and pied hens can have as large and as bright cheek

Male courtship sequence. Platinum Pearl pair.

patches as cocks of their mutation.

The general rule is that sexually mature cocks in the normal grey cockatiels and all mutations that involve a colour change only, without a feather pattern change, have a bright well- defined yellow mask, solidly coloured tail feathers and no juvenile under wing spots when fully mature.

Mature hens have tinges of yellow in varying intensity around their eyes and beak, their under tail feathers are yellow, barred with their body colour. Their cheek patches are generally muted with their body colour also, making them appear less bright. They also retain the underwing spots though some birds occasionally fledge without these.

Young birds resemble mature hens with pink toned ceres and shorter tails and crests. They begin a juvenile moult at approximately four months of age, lasting about two months, when cocks begin to develop their yellow faces. They will often drop some of their tail feathers which will then be replaced with solid coloured tail feathers in cock birds. The hens will produce new barred tail feathers.

Above: Courtship behaviour. Hen is inviting the cock bird to mate.
Left: Mating.

Some families are slower than others to mature and changes to facial feathers may not be noticeable by four months of age. If this happens I may pull a barred tail feather to speed the process up a little. However, if the feather is pulled prior to four months of age, it may be replaced with another juvenile tail feather, giving you a false impression of their gender.

Behaviour is also one of the methods of sexing birds, in fact, with pieds and lutinos it is often the best and possibly only indication to go by. Healthy active young cocks will commence singing and chortling to themselves as early as eight weeks of age. Cocks will be seen lifting their shoulders while they flatten out their wings and cross the tips. While doing this they often appear to be doing a little 'soft shoe shuffle' from side to side, combined with repetitive singing. Some cocks raise and lower their bodies in a bowing motion to the hens while they lift their shoulders. Others follow the hen of their choice endlessly around the aviary, making little hops or skips as they go. The hen usually appears oblivious to the cock's attentions unless she wishes to mate, then she crouches down with her tail elevated, and makes a twittering sound.

Hens can sometimes sing as well as young cocks and I have also seen hens mating other hens, which certainly complicates sex determination. I have never heard of anyone who has witnessed the shoulder lifting behaviour in a hen, so if the colouring of the bird does not reveal its sex I consider this activity to be the next most accurate way of identifying cocks.

A problem that arises when attempting to determine the gender of pied birds is that you can only make the assumption that a bird is a hen by the fact that you have not witnessed it behaving like a cock. There is always room for error if the bird is a slow maturing cock, or if you are not able to observe your birds for signs of male behaviour all day.

Lutino hens are expected to show yellow underwing spots on a creamy white background but I do not feel that this is an accurate method of sexing lutinos as it is dependant on the bird having enough yellow and white contrast for these spots to be visible. If the bird is also pearl or pied the normal wing spot pattern will be disrupted and this theory of sex determination will no longer apply.

Cock lutinos develop a hormonal overlay at maturity that appears as very pale brownish or mauve tinge to their wings that does not penetrate into the white wing bar. Hens never develop this colouration.

There are many other theories based on pelvic bones and cheek patches, all of which are at least 50% accurate. Many breeders may now have access to surgical sexing but it is not a practice that we have found necessary to use for cockatiels. Our birds rarely leave our aviaries until they have completed their juvenile moult and are better equipped to handle the stress of transport. In addition, surgical sexing in very young birds is stressful and can be inaccurate so, by the time a bird is old enough for the procedure to be safe and accurate, one should be able to determine the bird's sex by a bit of patient observation.

Compatibilty

Cockatiels will breed at any time of the year if given the opportunity. The fact that they will do so does not mean that they should, nor that they will produce young of the same quality all year round. As our interest is in producing quality birds and protecting our valuable breeding stock we make the decisions as to when they should be allowed to breed. The onset of spring generally triggers the breeding urge and this is also the safest period for both parents and young.

Cockatiels, when allowed to choose their own mate, will form a strong pair bond and usually require no coaxing to breed. While this may seem ideal it is rare that your choice of an ideal partner for a particular bird is the same as their choice. More often than not they form a bond with a sibling.

We commonly practise our personal version of line breeding to develop the characteristics we desire and to establish good quality birds but rarely would we practise inbreeding. We consider brother to sister, mother to son and father to daughter combinations inbreeding. In many cases this type of mating rapidly results in loss of fertility, loss of breeding urge, increased incidence of baldness regardless of the mutation variety, loss of size and generally produces less hardy birds. LOSS is the overwhelming result of uncontrolled breeding.

Ideally then, we choose partners for our birds on paper first, working out the best genetic pairings and also taking into consideration the individual characteristics of the birds such as size, conformation, temperament, depth of colour and so on. After determining the pairs we allow them to spend the winter together when the breeding urge is lowest. Winter is an ideal time to build up the birds for the coming breeding season. In addition, pairs that are not immediately compatible will often form a bond by the time the season approaches and you have enough time to choose an alternative partner for any that are obviously incompatible. While the latter situation is rare, it does happen.

Although cockatiels will breed in winter, there can be many disadvantages in doing so. The hens, particularly young hens, are more prone to egg binding in cold weather. Any night fright will cause the total loss of eggs and young in a relatively short period and the shorter daylight hours will allow less time for the parents to feed the young. The results are chicks that are generally smaller, fledge later than normal, a higher loss rate in younger chicks and a higher incidence of nutritional disorders such as calcium deficiency.

Nest Boxes & Mating

Compatible pairs receive a nest box in early August. As it is still winter, hens should be watched closely for signs of egg binding if they commence laying shortly thereafter. The benefit of this timing is that chicks commence hatching in spring when conditions are becoming milder and the light hours increase as the feeding requirements of the young increase. In addition, a second round of young can be raised before the height of summer, avoiding possible losses in the nest caused by excessive heat.

In Western Australia we generally remove nest boxes after the second round and if a third is desired then the boxes can be replaced when the weather begins to cool. In Tasmania summer heat has seldom caused a stressful problem. Likewise, winter cold is not usually extreme enough to cause breeding problems in mature, experienced pairs in peak condition who are determined to breed. Youngsters bred in winter have fledged as early and as large a fledging as those bred in other seasons.

The use of extended timed lighting (16 hours per day) and 18 Watt fluorescent night lights eliminate many of the disadvantages of winter breeding. Our Tasmanian aviaries are much more enclosed than those in Western Australia but no artificial heat is used. The very short winter days are the biggest adjustment to living so far south. Extended lighting allows the birds extra eating and exercise time during winter. Their aviaries have polycarbonate panels overhead allowing each aviary sunlight whenever available. Hobart has some sunshine most days throughout the year. Rarely is an entire day overcast. Variations to these management practices occur throughout

Above:
Cockatiel nestbox.
Below:
Cockatiel nestbox with rear inspection hatch.

Australia due to the extreme changes in climate from north to south.

We choose to use larger nest boxes for our cockatiels than others recommend. This is primarily due to the fact that many of our clutches are quite large. Five or more large chicks in a nest can generate considerable heat, particularly when feathering up, and the larger dimensions of the boxes allow the chicks enough room to move apart and permits some air flow between them.

Our boxes hang vertically and they measure 450mm high (18 inches) and 250mm (10 inches) internally, squared. An entrance hole is cut near the top and a hardwood landing perch fixed below it. Two or three slats or steps are fixed internally to assist the parents to come and go without having to jump in on top of eggs. This also helps the youngsters practise climbing up and down before the big jump into the wide world. We stopped using wire ladders after some chicks were injured.

Boxes can be made of any untreated wood. Chipboard, plywood and craftwood are commonly used. The latter has some advantages in being perfectly smooth and it is easy to cut and glue edges. Mites have few places to hide in a craftwood box if the joins are filled with a non-toxic wood glue.

It is worthwhile making the effort to find hardwood pieces for the landing perch and steps leading into the nest box. Bored, incubating parents often chew away at chipboard steps, leaving the nailheads exposed. In the past a chick managed to impale itself on one of these exposed nailheads.

When nest boxes are to be mounted externally on suspended aviaries, the inspection hatch is at the back close to the level of the chicks. In the case of boxes hung inside the aviary the inspection hatch needs to be in front or on the side. We make our boxes with lids that can easily be propped open slightly in excessive heat. When using this method be sure to check the young to confirm that they are being fed. We have had some parents refuse to enter their nest if the lid or inspection hatch is open or even ajar.

Cover the bottom of the box with 50 to 70mm (2-3 inches) of firmly packed nesting material. Diana uses approximately two-thirds coarse hardwood sawdust to one-third pine shavings. Peggy uses medium coarse Tasmanian Oak shavings, with a good handful of precious Huon pine shavings, a natural insecticide, added. Shavings can be sifted through a 5mm (1/4 inch) screen, to remove as much dust as possible, before storing it to age. Whatever you choose to use be sure that your material does not come from wood treated with chemicals. The main criterion is that the nesting material should be absorbent but not too fine and dusty as this can clog the nares and mouths of the chicks.

Very dry materials, such as fine peat moss, are unsuitable because they absorb enough moisture to combat the hen's attempts to control humidity for her eggs.

All of our cockatiels breed in nest boxes. They are easier than logs to clean and move around and we have not experienced any difficulties in getting the birds to accept them.

Since the nest boxes are virtually identical few, if any, problems are ever encountered if a box has to be replaced during the breeding season.

Once the boxes are provided, bonded cockatiels are quick to inspect the nest box. The cock is usually the first to enter and if he considers the box to be safe and suitable he will often be heard singing inside in an effort to entice the hen to enter. Part of the ritual of accepting the nest box as a pair involves a lot of twittering discussion about remodelling and the entrance is often adjusted, but cockatiels are not usually destructive.

Above: Cinnamon hen. This hen was in egg laying cycle when photographed - indicated by slightly humped rump area.
Right: Cockatiel eggs in the nest.

If pairs are not given enough time to bond before being given a box, the hen may enter the box herself and commence laying and incubating before mating with the cock. If you observe that the cock is not taking his turn at sitting this may be the case. If there is a great deal of nest box and mating activity by both birds you can expect eggs as early as one week after hanging the box. Considerable digging and scratching activity in the nesting material usually signals the onset of egg laying.

Egg Laying and Incubation

Cockatiel eggs are white and normally about 25mm (1 inch) long. Five to seven eggs are usually laid on alternate days, however, some young hens will occasionally continue laying until the chicks hatch. I try to accustom all my birds to regular nest inspections and do so by quietly talking to the pair while gently rubbing on the inspection hatch before opening it. The birds often depart but some stay in the box moving to one side or rocking and hissing above their eggs. This is ideal if they calmly allow you to handle the eggs but parents who depart in fright when your hand enters the nest can scatter and dent their eggs. I try to slide my hand in so that the back of my hand is towards the adult bird and the eggs are shielded from damage if the bird becomes alarmed and leaves suddenly. After a few regular nest inspections most fully mature birds will calmly accept the inspection.

One benefit of nest inspection during egg laying is that it allows you to mark the eggs as they are laid and to candle the eggs for fertility. You will be able to predict exactly when the eggs should start to hatch. If a hen lays excessively, she will not be able to properly incubate all the eggs. By labelling the eggs with a non-toxic marker in the order that they were laid, you can remove the last eggs as they appear, provided that you have candled the first five or six eggs and found them to be fertile. It also allows you to recognise potential egg laying problems. If eggs do not appear when they are due or the eggs are abnormal in some way, watch the hen closely for signs of poor health.

Both parents share incubation duties that usually start in earnest with the laying of the third egg. However, some pairs commence incubation immediately with the hen usually incubating at night and the cock taking the day shift. Particularly enthusiastic hens will sometimes do both shifts and very devoted pairs will often incubate together. The cock does not feed the hen so both the hen and the cock will come off the nest from time to time to feed.

Problems with Incubation

Most young birds can be educated to be good parents with a little foresight and effort and a lot of trial and patience. We feel that it is better to try and educate your birds to be good parents than to train them to lay eggs for artificial incubation production or to give up and get rid of them. I always expect first time pairs to be less successful than older, experienced birds. Sometimes first nests are laid perfectly, incubated, fed and fledged. Birds that are closer to two years old instead of 'about' one year old when they attempt breeding are usually more successful with their first nest.

Unfortunately, when it comes to breeding, things don't always run smoothly and all too often our efforts to rectify the situation only make things worse. I have listed some common problems encountered during egg laying and incubation and some possible remedies.

Infertile or Clear Eggs

When attempting to breed with a young pair for the first time who lay and incubate perfectly but do not have fertile eggs replace a few of their clear eggs with fertile eggs from another pair. If they hatch and raise chicks together successfully their next round of eggs is usually fertile. Their hormone cycles seem to settle down and be synchronised for the next try. If you pull the eggs to stimulate another clutch of their own you may alter their brooding instinct and cause other incubation problems.

Infertile eggs can result from eager hens laying eggs before bonding and mating has occurred. If you suspect that this is the case remove the eggs and nest box for several weeks. This will allow them adequate time to get acquainted. If the cock is incubating, you can also try hatching fertile eggs under the pair, allowing them to raise a foster family. This should bring about the required hormonal activity and the next round of eggs is often fertile.

Hen Fails to Incubate Full Term

Inexperienced hens sometimes leave the nest prior to completion of incubation. Try replacing some of their eggs with eggs that are more advanced than their own that will commence pipping while the hen is still incubating. The realisation that young eventually hatch from the eggs will usually trigger the normally reliable cockatiel maternal instincts.

Hens That Fail to Incubate

This is a common problem with first time hens. They are best paired with an experienced cock who will incubate his shift regardless of the hen's activities. These hens often lay continuously as the lack of brooding instinct that usually terminates egg laying has resulted in the continuation of egg production hormones. If these hens are entering the box to lay and to sit intermittently with the cock bird, then a pipping egg from another pair can be placed in the nest while the cock is sitting. Again, the realisation that young are hatching often rectifies the situation and she may have no further problems. If the cock has not incubated during the night shift the eggs will have died. If they are important eggs I place clear eggs under the pair and artificially incubate the original eggs, placing them back under the pair as each one pips in the incubator.

Cocks Who Inspect the Box, Mate and Fertilise Eggs But Do Not Incubate

The same advice applies as with the hens though it is a little more difficult to correct because the cock has no reason to enter the box except to check on the hen. However, if you leave the hen sitting on clear eggs and artificially incubate the fertile ones, you can try hatching an egg under the hen. It is difficult primarily because many chicks hatch in the very early morning when the cock is due to take over. If the hen leaves the nest at day break and the cock does not take over, the chick could rapidly die from cold. If you want to try the exercise, you need to get up at day break and be ready to rescue the chick if the cock does not assume his fatherly duties.

I have had two cocks that do not incubate until they hear the hens feeding young. Then they become perfect fathers, brooding their young through the day and incubating and hatching the remaining eggs. Some hens will raise a clutch on their own though this is very difficult for the hen and she should not be left with a large number of young to raise alone.

During the breeding season there are often clear eggs being laid by unpaired hens. I collect these on a regular basis to have a supply of fresh eggs to use in emergencies such as those described above. Old eggs generally dry out and lose weight and are not suitable to use. Some specialist pet or bird dealers have very realistic polyurethane eggs that are perfect for substitution. These 'eggs' are similar in weight and size to cockatiel eggs and retain their brooding temperature just like normal eggs.

Feather Plucking

Feather plucking in the nest would be one of the most frustrating problems encountered by cockatiel breeders. There are no simple solutions to offer. The one thing we are certain of is that in some cases feather plucking is a learnt habit. Most birds that have been plucked as chicks will in turn pluck their own young. If you remove the chicks for hand raising as soon as plucking becomes evident you can certainly reduce the likelihood of future plucking. However, parents that have never been plucked will often, without warning, begin to pluck their chicks. Some will raise several clutches before the habit begins.

There are several different possible causes of the habit and it is impossible to find one solution. Last season one of my hens plucked the heads of her chicks as soon as she began to lay and incubate another round of eggs before the previous clutch had fledged. Whilst brooding this clutch the weather became quite hot so she wasn't inclined to lay another round of eggs and therefore, her current youngsters fledged and weaned without a feather out of place.

Other parents attack their chicks quite viciously without warning, removing many feathers and often inflicting small wounds in a single day. I am sure that this is done in an effort to drive the young out of the nest. One suggestion is to put in another nest box for the youngsters to use while fledging and the cock will feed them. This is not always successful, especially for cockatiels, because the cock bird would normally be in the nest box incubating during the day. Providing another nest box for the hen assumes that she will switch her chosen nesting box - my hens always seem to want to use the same box.

Above: Cockatiel chicks taken for handrearing due to feather plucking.
Right: Cockatiel chicks in the nest. These chicks all hatched within 60 hours, indicating that incubation did not begin until the fourth egg was laid.

I have noticed that hyperactive birds are more likely to pluck, particularly hens who must brood their chicks for long hours during the night. It could be that chicks with light coloured feathers may be more commonly plucked simply because their pin feathers are more visible in the darkness.

There may be a multitude of other causes that we are unaware of. At the moment the only solutions that I feel are effective to any degree comprise a good diet including minerals and trace elements, reduction of stress related environmental factors and breaking the cycle through hand raising.

Hatching

Incubation lasts eighteen to twenty-one days depending on when the pair begins to sit tightly and how warm the days are. Parents typically begin to sit tightly after the hen lays her third egg so that up to three babies can hatch on the one day. However, if temperatures are very warm, incubation can start almost immediately.

After the initial pip in most trouble free hatches, a chick emerges within 48 hours. If the chick takes longer than this to emerge you should watch closely for signs of difficulty. In hot dry weather, you are more likely to experience hatching difficulties due to the internal membrane drying. Hens regularly walk into their water dish in order to transport moisture into the nest. In very dry conditions she may not be able to keep the humidity up to the required level. This lack of moisture will cause the internal membrane to dry out and the chick will be unable to rotate freely to complete chipping out of the egg. If you suspect that pipping eggs are drying out you can moisten them morning and night with a clean cotton ball and some warm water that has been boiled and allowed to cool.

From top:
Cockatiel chick hatching sequence.

The hatching process involves the chick initially breaking through the membrane into the internal air cell when it begins to breathe air. This is referred to as the internal pip and from here the chick then dents the external shell which allows fresh air into the egg and the membrane begins to dry. The chick appears to work on one area for a minimum of 24-48 hours while the remaining yolk sac is drawn into the body. A chick that is strong and progressing normally can be heard tapping away inside the egg and usually begins to cheep on the second day.

If the chick is hatching normally, it will begin to chip the shell in a circular pattern as it rotates in the egg shell after the yolk absorption process is complete, breaking through the shell until the lid pops off. The chick struggles and kicks off the remaining shell. This rotation process should take no more than about ten minutes. It is disastrous to open an egg before the yolk sac has been absorbed, however, it is rare that the rotation process begins without absorption being complete. If you feel that the chick is making little progress when rotation has commenced, it is possible that it is stuck to the membrane and it is best to assist the hatching chick at this point.

Chicks that have taken a long time to emerge or have been assisted in hatching are often dehydrated and weak and have little chance of survival under the parents. They are best removed for hand rearing for 24-48 hours until they are strong enough to feed properly from their parents. When they can hold their head up to beg for food they can be safely returned to the nest. After hatching, all chicks should be observed in the evening and for the next few days to make sure they are strong enough to survive. No matter how good your parents are they can do little to help a chick that is unable to hold its head up to feed.

I have heard many people say that weak chicks should not be assisted to survive but I believe that if tchicks are weak only because of environmental factors in the nest then it is a waste to let these chicks die.

I have successfully assisted many chicks in difficulty that have grown into exceptional adults. If a chick has some of the yolk sac still outside the body after hatching, remove the chick immediately for hand raising. Do not pull or remove any of the sac and treat the area gently with a cotton bud and Betadine solution several times a day. In many cases, if the chick is kept on a clean soft surface such as facial tissues and infection is avoided, the yolk sac will eventually dry up and fall off.

Artificial Incubation

Although we are great believers in educating breeding birds to be good parents, our incubators run continuously throughout the breeding season. Last season only a handful of chicks were raised from the egg; however for a variety of reasons, many eggs passed through the incubators and quite a few of last season's young are here only because of the incubators! When breeding mutations one often has only younger, inexperienced birds to use, and the incubator is helpful in sorting out incubation problems. Eggs won't be lost through irregular incubation and can often be ultimately hatched under the parents, solving the problem on a permanent basis. Hens laying thin shelled eggs that are frequently damaged can have their eggs brought to hatching in the incubator and then returned to them if clear or artificial eggs have been left for them to continue their natural cycle of incubation. Chicks with hatching difficulties can be watched more closely in the incubator and assisted in hatching if need be. These chicks can remain in the incubator while being fed until they are strong enough to be placed under the parents.

If necessity dictates, I will hand raise from the egg but only when no alternative can be found. It is a long and tedious task that can be both rewarding and terribly frustrating.

I use two fan forced incubators. One contains eggs developing from day one to pipping. It is set at 37.6°C (99.75°F) with a wet bulb reading of 27.75°C (82°F). The incubator is equipped with an automatic turning device that turns the eggs 180° every half hour. Eggs should not be automatically turned for the last three days of incubation or after the internal pip has taken place. This can be determined by candling, though if you are not sure then you can wait until the first dent appears on the outside of the eggshell. At this point, I transfer the egg to a hatching incubator. This has a much higher humidity level and a slightly lower temperature and the automatic turning mechanism is disengaged.

Above: Whiteface cockatiel chick at 11 days.
Right: Cockatiel chick at approximately 3 weeks. Whiteface Cinnamon Pearl.
Below: Cockatiel chicks at approximately 3 weeks. Cinnamon Pearl, Whiteface Pearl and Whiteface Cinnamon Pearl.

The wet bulb thermometer should read at least 34.4°C (94°F) and the temperature should be 36.9°C (98.5°F). This information is only very basic and based on our personal methods. Anyone wishing to try incubation on a regular basis should consult more detailed texts on the procedure. Eggs should be marked and dated for identification purposes and when young hatch, they should also be clearly identified.

Incubators can be used to increase the

yield of rare or valuable birds. However, the practice of continuously pulling eggs can result in future breeding problems for a pair that may otherwise have been good reliable parents. I have bred successfully from incubator hatched, hand raised birds, but never allowing cockatiel parents to raise their own young may result in generations of birds that lack the skills to do so. On the other hand, I rarely have problems with any birds that have been hatched and raised by very good parents. They seem to inherit their parents' skills.

Chick Development

Chicks grow rapidly for the first three weeks, often reaching two-thirds of their adult body weight by the time they are two weeks old. Pin feathers begin to show as early as seven days and chicks should be fully feathered by four weeks of age. Feather development appears to be governed by the growth rate of the chick.

Often the youngest chick will not require banding nor show signs of pin feathers until two weeks of age, taking a full week longer than the oldest chick to reach the same stage. These chicks should be closely monitored, as growth abnormalities and stunting can result in a chick that falls far behind. Hand raising these chicks may help them survive but it can rarely reverse the damage caused in the early stages if they are taken too late. If a slow growing chick is recognised before permanent stunting occurs the use of a good hand raising diet will help it catch up to its nest mates.

Hand raising can sometimes be avoided by transferring young from one nest to another. This should only be done where accurate records are kept and identification of the young is in no doubt. For instance, if a pair hatches a fifth and sixth chick, these often end up in difficulty within a short period of time. They will either die or require hand raising, as they are too small to compete with the oldest chicks for food.

If you have several pairs breeding at the same time you can often place the two youngest from a nest of six with the youngest from another nest, removing two of their older chicks. The more advanced chicks can be placed with the older chicks from the first nest. The idea is to have all the young birds in the nest about the same size so they can compete more effectively for food.

Closed banded chicks can easily be identified but unbanded chicks must be marked clearly so there is no question about their origin. Their rumps can be marked with a non-toxic water based marker, though this needs to be checked morning and night and renewed as necessary until they are old enough to be close banded. Any movement of chicks from one nest to another needs to be done gradually, one at a time, so that you are sure that the chick has been accepted and that the parents do not abandon their young.

Chicks that appear to be falling behind can also be assisted by filling their crops for them first thing in the morning with a good hand raising mix. Small chicks are weakest when their crops have been empty for some time. They are also the last to be fed, sometimes waiting several hours for a feed while the parents fill the oldest chicks first. This weakens them even more until they may be too weak to ask for food. Giving them a feed will give them the boost that they need in order to compete for food and will at least sustain them until their parents get around to feeding them.

Feeding chicks in the nest can be a slow and painstaking operation. They are not used to a spoon, so the food needs to be quite runny and warm to get them to accept it. As you will rarely get a normal feeding response, you need to feed small amounts to reduce the risk of the chick inhaling the mix and suffocating.

Our birds are all accustomed to regular nest inspections and, when young are in the nest, chicks are checked morning and night. Droppings build up rapidly in the nest and occasionally a chick will get its vent or beak blocked by dried droppings. This is rapidly fatal in either case so all chicks are given a quick top and tail check to ensure that both are clear.

A chick that has a pasted over vent needs to be watched closely for signs of possible diarrhoea that may either have caused the problem or may be the result of the problem. A blocked vent can rapidly cause peritonitis. A chick that has its beak clogged with droppings may have been without food for many hours and may need a liquid feed to help it regain its strength.

Chicks should also be monitored for normal leg development. If your breeding birds are supplied with a good nutritious diet, a plentiful supply of calcium and minerals and nest boxes have adequate nesting material, this should rarely be a problem. However, any abnormalities such as splayed legs or injuries that may occur need immediate attention if they are to heal adequately. One solution we have heard recommended for splayed legs is to band the chick on both legs and to connect both bands together with a paper clip, thus holding the legs underneath the chick's body while still allowing growth.

By the end of each day chicks should have full crops but the contents should feel neither excessively dry nor excessively wet. Either of these conditions could signal a potential problem with the chick.

As the chicks approach four weeks of age, the amount of food found each evening in their crop begins to reduce as the chicks slim down in anticipation of fledging. Once the young have fledged they need to be watched to ensure that they are still being fed and that they have sustained no injuries in their initial 'crash bang' efforts of flying.

Young cockatiels will usually be independent by seven to eight weeks of age but should not be removed from their parents until all signs of begging have ceased. Chicks will appear to be husking seed shortly after fledging, but in many cases they are only imitating their parents and are not actually swallowing any seed.

Hand Rearing

Hand rearing is something that all bird keepers will face at some stage in their hobby. Whether or not as a result of artificial incubation, assisting weak chicks, taking slow or feather plucked chicks or just to imprint young birds for pets it need not be difficult for you. Although time consuming, provided several essential requirements are catered for adequately, it shouldn't be life threatening to the chicks.

The basic requirements for hand rearing young cockatiels are:

Hygiene

Regardless of the age of the chicks, poor hygiene will ultimately result in problems. Incubator hatched young are without the benefits of their parents' antibodies and digestive enzymes in their crop. Until they develop their own immunities they are highly susceptible to bacterial infections. Incubators and brooders require regular cleaning and disinfection and the nursery itself needs to be kept as clean as

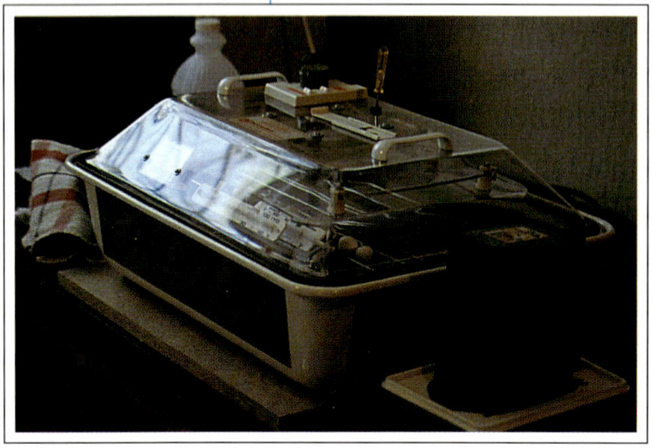

Above: One of the incubators we use.
Right: Accurate thermostatically controlled brooder.
Below: Handraising equipment.

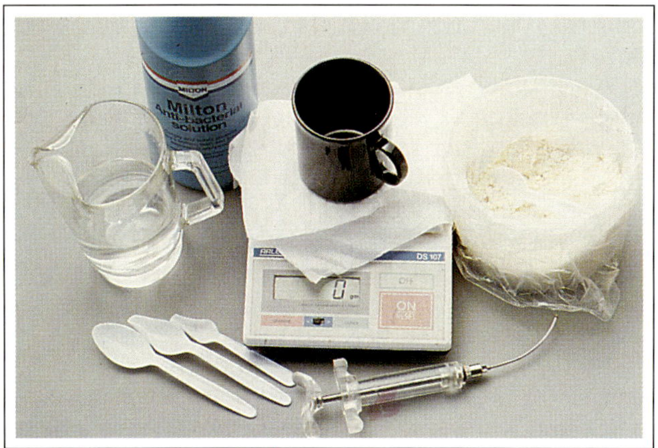

possible.

We recommend keeping chicks that are beginning to feather in a different room from incubators and brooders containing very small chicks. Dust from discarded feather casings is produced in large amounts and spread enthusiastically by chicks practising to fly. Not only is the dust a health hazard to very young chicks but it is potentially damaging to the sensitive mechanics of incubators and brooders.

All feeding implements and mixing cups need to be sterilised prior to use. Submerge feeding cups and spoons in Milton™ infant sterilising solution at the recommended strength. At the start of each day also submerge a water jug for the recommended time. Then rinse out the jug with boiling water a few times before filling it with boiled water to cool.

When about to feed rinse the mixing cup and spoons with boiling water and cool before mixing the food. This is done to remove the antibacterial solution from the feeding utensils to avoid the chicks ingesting some of the solution. Although this is not required for human babies we feel that it is a sound practice with baby birds as antibacterial solution in their crops could predispose chicks to fungal infections. Digestion requires the presence of friendly bacteria in the crop. Destruction of these bacteria can upset the delicate balance in the crop and result in growth of yeast fungus.

We use disposable plastic spoons for both mixing and feeding. These spoons can be easily bent into the correct shape for feeding by submerging them in boiling water for a short time and pinching the sides together when the plastic has softened.

Below: Cockatiel chicks at 3-5 days. Two Whiteface one Normal (yellow down).

After each feeding the lining of the containers housing the chicks is changed. In the case of very small chicks, use a bed of soft facial tissues. With larger chicks use a bed of shredded computer paper covered with paper towelling. The containers are also replaced with clean sterile ones each day or as required. While these practices are not as necessary for older chicks that have been taken from the nest, we feel that it is better to be 'safe than sorry', as the struggle to save a chick that has become ill is a heartbreaking experience.

The hand-rearing formula should always be mixed fresh with cooled boiled water for each feed. Use separate batches of food and fresh feeding implements for each group of chicks. In this way a bacterial, viral or fungal problem can be prevented from spreading through your nursery before it is detected.

Diet

We have the utmost respect for anyone that successfully raised chicks prior to the arrival of the new range of avian hand rearing formulas now available. It was certainly more difficult to hand raise young cockatiels than it is now. There are several excellent formulas on the market that take all the guess work out of feeding chicks. They are highly digestible, totally balanced diets requiring nothing other than the addition of water and warmth. When fed according to the manufacturer's directions you should be able to raise youngsters with weaning weights equivalent to and in some cases better than those of parent raised chicks.

The most important rule with these commercial foods is to feed them as directed. Many people mix one brand with another and add different ingredients that may ultimately result in digestion problems and will certainly alter the guaranteed nutrition. While some species of parrots may need additives in order to attain optimum growth rates, we have found no problems raising cockatiels without altering the formula.

A set of accurate scales for weighing the ingredients makes it easier to mix the correct consistency of formula relative to the age of the chicks. Inexpensive digital kitchen scales which read in 1 or 2 gram increments, are available from electrical appliance stores. Scales that are accurate to 0.1 gram are far better if you are raising tiny chicks requiring very dilute formula but the cost of these can be prohibitive.

Hand rearing formulas differ mostly in the fat content. If raising very young chicks use Roudybush™ Formula 3 Handfeeding Mix. The higher fat content gives better initial weight gain, though chicks raised on Roudybush™ may be a little more inclined to digestion problems if the formula is not mixed to the correct consistency or not enough care has been taken with hygiene. At the first sign of digestion slowing, immediately switch to a mix with a lower fat content such as Vetafarm™ Parrot Hand Rearing Food and feed a more dilute mix containing Nilstat™ anti fungal drops for human babies until the problem has cleared. Older chicks that have completed most of their growth cycle appear to accept the Vetafarm™ mix easily and adapt to the spoon very quickly. As it digests very rapidly, we recommend that inexperienced people try using this mix. Vetafarm™ has changed the formulation of their hand raising food as of the 1994-95 breeding season.

Temperature of the formula is also extremely important. I have a jug with boiled water cooled from the previous feeding. To this I add boiling water to bring the temperature up again, however, never add water that is boiling or close to boiling to the formula. With some mixes this has the effect of cooking the mix and altering its digestibility. I then test the food against the inside of my wrist. It should feel warm but never hot as the sensitive lining of the mouth and crop can be easily burned.

If the mixture has gone too cold by the time it has swelled to its final consistency, you can heat it for a couple of seconds in the microwave or rest the cup in a bowl of boiling water for a short time. Formula that has been reheated must be thoroughly stirred and the temperature retested before feeding to ensure that there are no hot spots. Chicks will refuse to eat formula that is cold and if they ingest food that is too cool it can have the effect of chilling the chick, thus increasing the likelihood of it becoming ill.

Temperature and Humidity

The younger the chicks, the more crucial temperature and humidity are. Tiny chicks are unable to tolerate temperature fluctuations and need to be kept in as stable an environment as possible. An incubator will suffice while the chick dries out but many are fan forced and the chick may suffer if it remains in an environment where the air is blowing directly on to it. There are several commercial brooders on the market that have accurate thermostats, though some are not as well designed in other areas, such as ease of cleaning.

If the chicks are over a week old you can manage with a hospital box fitted with two 25 watt bulbs and a dimmer switch. The benefit of having two bulbs is that the chicks will probably survive the drop in temperature if only one bulb fails. On the other hand, if there is only one bulb in the box and it fails, they can rapidly die before the problem is noticed. Dimmer switches do not prevent the temperature in the box from gradually rising and gradually declining as the room temperature fluctuates throughout the day and night. Without a thermostat the heat level will require constant monitoring and adjustment.

Thermometers are best placed in the container that holds the chick as sometimes conditions inside the container can vary several degrees from the environment outside the container. 'Tandy Electronics' markets a handy inexpensive digital thermometer that has a probe on the end of a long cord. The probe can easily be positioned into the container while the thermometer itself remains outside the brooder for easy reading. Be sure that the chicks are not actually leaning against the probe itself or you will have abnormally high readings. Recommended brooding temperatures are as follows, though parent raised chicks that are taken at two weeks or older often seem to find these temperatures too high:

35-37°C	(96-99°F)	- Week 1
32.5°C	(90°F)	- Week 2
27°C	(80°F)	- Week 3

Decreases in temperature should be gradual over a 48 hour period. The chicks themselves should be monitored by their behaviour and their droppings and not just by the temperature. Chicks should not shiver, nor should they sit apart from each other and pant. Contented chicks will normally sleep for hours between feeds in a little heap with their necks crossed over each other. The youngest chick is always cuddled up underneath and in the centre of the warm bodies. It is much more difficult to keep an individual chick content as it has no one else to snuggle up to for comfort. I've made tiny chicks little blankets of the super fleece fabric used for tracksuits. Just for cuddling, not for covering!

If temperatures are too high as the formula is gradually thickened, dehydration can occur and the first signs of this can be seen in the droppings. Normal droppings should be well-formed but they should not be at all dry. If droppings are not accompanied by a reasonable amount of liquid, monitor your conditions carefully.

Older chicks beginning to pin feather are much easier to cater for. I feel that the best environment for these chicks is to house them in plastic boxes such as the ones you can buy for storage. The containers should be large enough to position a heat source on one side and should have a firm base, such as shredded paper, covered with paper towelling. Over the top you can place a towel, leaving the top end opposite the heat source open. Place a thermometer in the box to ensure that the environment is within an acceptable temperature range. The chicks can then move closer to or further away from the heat source as required and the environment is very easy to clean and disinfect.

We prefer electric foot warmers as a gentle source of heat without added stress from continual light. Small heating pads are generally used in foot warmers. Some come in a flannelette casing that you are meant to put your feet into. This can be removed, exposing the plastic covered pad for easy cleaning. Kambrook™ have a foot warmer covered with a soft carpet type fabric. It can also be removed for cleaning. The Kambrook™ appliance is larger than most and is designed to tilt but is easy to use for many bird purposes. I often set small boxes or holding cages partially on it for heat support. Small lamps fitted with a dimmer switch and coloured bulbs can be easily used for extra heat, with adequate protection. The most important thing to remember is that a growing chick must be allowed the freedom to explore its area away from the warmth or cuddle up safely to the heat source.

I once looked at a happy little bird and was told that it had been hand raised alone. The heat source used was a 40 watt bulb. After being fed the chick had leaned on the globe for warmth and cooked its bulging crop and contents enough so that when it pulled away the top of its crop tore from its body. The breeder, a nurse, was understandably shocked but quickly grabbed household needle and thread and stitched it up, after carefully taking out the contents. The bird did not seem to suffer and fledged with no obvious sign of the injury. This true story made a huge impression on me as a new bird keeper.

Any brooder that you may use requires humidity to prevent dehydration in the young. This can be provided by placing a dish of water close to the heat source. A dish 80-100mm (3-4 inches) across is usually adequate. With older chicks kept in plastic tubs there is generally enough moisture being produced by their droppings at this stage not to require additional humidity but it is still best to monitor your chicks for signs of dry skin and dehydration.

When and How to Feed

Some experts advise that newly hatched chicks should not be fed for up to 12 hours after hatching. This advice is suitable only if the youngsters hatch normally with no problems. Chicks that have had a difficult hatch often need immediate help. I have found that the safest way to help them is to feed only an electrolyte solution for the first 8 hours. The one I use is Gastrolyte™ natural flavour, available from chemists. This solution gives the chicks the energy they require without interfering with the remaining internal yolk absorption. It is also of great benefit to chicks that have become dehydrated in the egg and for these I continue adding Gastrolyte™ to their formula for up to 5 days. Dehydrated chicks are born with dry, reddish skin and have a bony, pinched look about them. If not properly rehydrated they do very poorly throughout their growth cycle.

Above: Spoon feeding.

Gastrolyte™ comes in sachets and should be mixed per the directions in a sterile container using boiled and cooled water. It must be kept in the fridge between feeds and discarded after 24 hours.

Chicks are fed every 1½-2 hours for the first 3 days except through the night. I feed at midnight, 3am and 6am and then back to the two hour schedule. On the fourth night they go from midnight to 6am without a feed. As the food thickens and the crop increases in capacity, feedings can be spread further apart and should be based on the crop size. Chicks should be fed when at least three-quarters of the crop contents have been digested.

Regularly scheduled feeds should continue throughout the day until about 11 pm but chicks should not be fed in the morning until the crop has emptied from the night before. If this takes too long, the chick may draw the remaining moisture out of the crop, making the contents thicken to where they cannot be digested. In this case I feel that it is better to feed a couple of diluted feeds and gently massage the crop contents so that the compacted food can break up and digest.

If the crop has become pendulous, usually a result of overfeeding, it will not empty and the chick will simply starve to death while you wait. In these circumstances it is better, I feel, to continue feeding but to massage the contents of the crop gently with each feed so that some of the old food digests and passes out through the digestive system with the new.

Nilstat™ should also be used for this situation. Old food lying in the

bottom of a crop undigested is a perfect breeding climate for the fungus *candida albicans*, the cause of thrush. Forcibly emptying the crop is often recommended for slow digestion, either by syringe or tipping the bird upside down and milking the contents out. It has been our experience that this procedure is disastrous with cockatiels, usually resulting in a worsening of the situation. Suspected bacterial infections are best treated by an avian vet who will administer the correct antibiotic at the correct dose.

As chicks approach fledging they are usually down to four meals a day, showing least interest in the morning meal and most in the evening meal. Some will only take a reasonable feed in the evening and this is no cause for concern as long as they appear bright and well. After fledging their appetite usually returns to normal.

Chicks that are taken by choice, not by necessity, are best taken at three weeks of age. At this time they will generally adapt quickly to the spoon and are not as delicate as younger chicks.

Above:
Weaning cage fitted with a Crompton Fire Lamp™
Below:
Weaning cage has an elevated wire base to allow droppings to fall through.

Chicks that are closer to fledging can be difficult to feed as they are not as hungry and can be very stubborn. If they open their mouth to hiss at you, you can quickly spoon a little food into their mouth. If they just sit and glare at you, have patience. We have had them go up to two and a half days without a reasonable feed. In situations such as this we often have success by sitting quietly with the chick, stroking it until it loses its fear. Placing it with younger chicks that are feeding well can often bring about a feeding response also. There is little choice with chicks that have already fledged other than to feed them with a crop needle.

I normally feed with a spoon from day one, rather than a syringe or a tube. I find it the safest and most natural way to feed, being similar to normal parent feeding. There are less weaning difficulties with spoon-fed chicks than with tube or syringe fed chicks, and less likelihood of the young inhaling the food if you are inexperienced.

If you choose to use a syringe or tube method for hand raising, plan to teach the young birds to eat from a spoon at about three weeks of age. This will stimulate their natural feeding response and they will wean more quickly and safely. If they eat from a spoon you cannot overfeed them when they prefer to reduce their food intake prior to fledging. Overfeeding at this age can then result in regurgitation simply because they are too full. Cockatiels should never regurgitate as youngsters. If you see this action, immediately suspect a health problem and get help.

Weaning

It is a common practice amongst people hand feeding chicks to reduce the number of feeds when they feel it is the appropriate time, in an effort to force chicks to wean. It has been my experience that cockatiels can be 'forced' to do very little at all. The reduction of food seldom helps chicks wean and more frequently results in hungry, insecure and distressed chicks. They become dangerously thin and obsessed with being fed and once they begin to behave in this manner, weaning becomes very difficult and drawn-out.

The process of weaning stems from the natural curiosity of the chicks picking up, nibbling and exploring things in their environment. In happy, contented chicks, this process commences in the nest box. After fledging the chicks learn from parents and companions that have already weaned.

Branches and seeding grasses are most readily accepted for nibbling. A bowl of dry seed and fresh water should always be available from the time the chicks fledge. Hand raised chicks always investigate seed and other bits scattered on the floor prior to fledging. Vegetables, particularly corn on the cob, also help the weaning process, giving the chicks something to nibble on. In this way they experience taste and swallowing follows shortly after. Chicks that suddenly have their food intake reduced before having learnt to swallow can become panicky and insecure and cease to explore their environment, choosing instead to sit and listen for the sound of your approach, begging constantly.

Hand feeding chicks can be a tedious process and the desire to wean the chicks for our own convenience becomes very strong. To alleviate this problem without starving the chicks, I choose instead to teach the chicks to eat off a plate in their 6th or 7th week. This is easily done by lowering the spoon into the bowl of food as the chicks are begging. You can encourage the chicks by feeding small mouthfuls from just above the level of the food, causing them to lower their heads and grab small mouthfuls of food. Once they understand where the food is, I leave the spoon in the bowl and quickly leave the room.

As long as the chicks are old enough, they usually learn to feed off the plate after two or three feeds. Always check their crops on returning to the room to make sure they have been adequately filled. The chicks can be fed four times a day with minimal inconvenience to the foster parents (us) when they learn to feed off a plate. They can eat their fill at their leisure and maintain their happy contented disposition, and their foster parent can maintain a happier disposition also. It appears to speed up the association with bending down and picking up small amounts of food as part of the weaning process in contrast to bending their heads back and receiving food rapidly from the spoon. The hand raising mix should be quite thick, similar to the consistency of porridge, for plate feeding.

Chicks will frequently wean much more rapidly on to soft food such as sprouts. Be sure that they are also eating dry seed, as you cannot know that they will be fed soft food for the rest of their lives. In addition, eating only sprouts can predispose chicks to future fungal infections.

Chicks lose considerable weight during the weaning process. As a bit of extra support I give my juveniles access to a heat source day and night in cooler weather until they have weaned and gained considerable weight. I build special weaning cages of all wire mesh approximately 600mm square by 800mm long. I fit a small wire box containing a hanging light bulb at one end, away from the food and water dishes. I use a 60 watt Crompton Fire Lamp™ for this purpose. These are orange coloured bulbs used for artificial fireplaces. The orange light is not disturbing at night but gives off more heat than red party bulbs that are only 40 watts. The wire box surrounding the light bulb is to prevent the chicks from chewing on the electrical wires and to prevent burns.

A variety of perches are secured around the light so several chicks can access the light at the same time or move away as required. A nest box can be hung on the side of the cage, allowing the chicks to fledge naturally in their own time into the cage. The base of the cage sits in a tray but is suspended 50mm (2 inches) above the tray to allow their droppings and spoiled food to fall through.

I reach into the cage and spoon feed the young, feeding several chicks at one time. This saves time and keeps them interested with the competition of their perch mate also eating. When the chicks get older they are easily distracted and get too busy to eat their fill without stopping for a little break to investigate something else. Feeding them inside the cage prevents the dangerous thrill of flying around the room, and into windows, with full crops.

Pet Cockatiels

Cockatiels as pets are more content when kept as pairs rather than as a solitary bird which is unnatural for a flock species. Without regular attention and companionship these intelligent birds will often become frustrated and develop behavioural problems such as shrieking for attention, or feather plucking. In theory we become the bird's flock and therefore replace its need for companionship. The reality is that the novelty of owning a tame bird can quickly wear thin and the bird spends more and more time confined to a cage, the size of which is the equivalent of a human being locked in a bathroom. When I refer to a pair of pet birds I mean two birds, not necessarily male and female, a true pair should be avoided if you do not wish to breed.

Housing, diet and other aspects of management relevant to keeping these birds as pets, have been covered elsewhere in this book. This brings me to some of the fallacies such as - *'If I have two birds they will not remain tame'*.

If you acquire two birds that have both been hand raised, and handle them frequently, there is no reason to expect them to revert to being wild. Hand raised budgies prefer their bird friends but cockatiels can easily share their affections with you and a feathered friend.

Personalities vary greatly in cockatiels and not all birds make good pets. A breeder should be able to supply you with a pet that comes from a particularly gregarious and friendly family. These birds, when hand raised, often remain tame even when placed in aviary situations with mates that are not tame. If you purchase a bird that is not tame as a companion for an existing pet, I recommend taming the second bird before introducing the two to each other. The fear that the new bird experiences will be felt by your existing bird and may alarm it. Many people who have acquired a hand raised bird from me as a companion for an existing pet have reported that the personality of their first bird had blossomed with the introduction of the new tame bird.

'If I have two birds I will not be able to teach them to talk.' The ability to mimic and the desire to do so varies from bird to bird with cocks usually more inclined to learn words. I do not teach my birds

to talk but one of my cocks taught himself to 'wolf whistle' and to make a noise resembling 'Donald Duck'. Being a very gregarious and vocal cock bird he managed to teach all my other cocks and some of my hens to make the same noise. I am quite sure that if I repeated words to him continuously, he would learn to talk and probably teach many birds in my flock to say the same words. Many reports have come back to me about pet birds learning to talk or whistle a particular tune.

As far as which sex makes a better pet, both have attributes that make them ideal. Cocks have a tendency to be very gregarious and entertaining, though many are not happy to be stroked and scratched but prefer to ride around on your head or shoulder, displaying a little gender domination. Hens, on the other hand, are very sweet and affectionate and will often gently insist that you scratch their heads for hours on end. They are frequently content to nuzzle into your neck and sit quietly for long periods.

Young cockatiels lose weight during the weaning process and can become ill if placed under stress such as being transported to a new home, pet shop or bird dealer. I therefore prefer to sell my pets after they have put on some weight and I am sure they are eating well on their own. They also need to be handled after they have weaned to learn to go to their handler for company and not just for food. Cockatiels that have been hand raised will be tame and confiding to the person who has raised them but can still be wary of strangers. There are some important steps to take when first introducing young birds to their new home.

I always send my birds to their new home with some of the seed they are accustomed to and a sheet containing details of their care and diet. I recommend that the birds remain confined to their cage for at least a day until they become accustomed to the voices and appearance of their new owners and the sounds of their new environment, especially any new animals. If there are several children in the family I recommend only one adult and one child at a time work with the birds. A room crowded with unfamiliar people can panic birds.

The birds should be kept in a smallish room initially and allowed to come out of the cage on their own if possible, or be encouraged to hop onto your hand and be lifted out. Do not chase them around the cage, as they may learn to fear you. Birds that are allowed to come out and explore their environment without fear will quickly become accustomed to their surroundings and their new owners. The smallish room prevents them from flying too fast and possibly injuring themselves or becoming alarmed by objects in the room.

If they initially fly away from you and land on the curtain rail, allow them to settle before quietly approaching them and encouraging them onto your hand. I always recommend having some eucalyptus or seeding grasses to occupy them while you have them in your lap or on your hand. As well as being a treat, it gives a nervous bird something to do and has a calming effect on them. As they become accustomed to you and their new surroundings, they will become increasingly bold and can be allowed to explore larger areas in the house. However, unless you clip a wing, it is best to restrict the birds to rooms that do not open directly to the outside of the house. I have had far too many calls from people who have lost their pet from walking directly outside with a bird perched on their shoulder. As soon as a bird discovers that it is in unfamiliar territory it usually takes flight in panic and is lost within a short time.

Sudden loud noises will alarm your birds, particularly telephones and doorbells. Stoves, sinks and refrigerators are potential death traps for pet cockatiels. If possible, draw curtains and close doors to the kitchen and toilet areas. Potentially poisonous house plants, the household cat or dog and toxic insect sprays are just a few other hazards to watch out for. The most important thing to remember for your pet's safety is simply to be aware of your birds and what they are doing while they are out of their safe cage and playing in your environment. With a little care you should experience years of companionship from these charming little birds.

Pet Cages

People who design the bird cages sold in pet stores seem to have little understanding or knowledge of the requirements of the eventual inhabitants. Each year I see cages become taller, narrower and less suitable, although they may seem more attractive from a decor point of view. Birds fly in a more or less horizontal fashion. Cockatiels fly rapidly up and down only when responding to a sudden fright. Therefore, cages that are longer and wider than their height are much more suitable for pet birds than tall, decorative styles.

Cockatiels that are tame and confiding to their owners can usually be released to fly at liberty in an area of the house. If they are allowed to explore and exercise freely for a period each day, the size of the cage is less critical to their health. For a pet cockatiel allowed regular exercise we would advise the minimum size cage to be 45cm x 45cm (18in x 18in).

A small cockatoo cage approximately 60cm x 60cm (2 feet x 2 feet) would allow two pet cockatiels to be housed comfortably, however, care must be taken not to leave cages of this type outside unattended. Cockatiels can comfortably put their heads through the bars and as a result are in danger of losing them to owls, hawks and cats. Cages with horizontal bars are more suitable for cockatiels to climb around on than the usual vertical bars used in canary cages.

When people purchase pets from me I frequently assist them to make their own cage from aviary weldmesh, using 'J' clips to fasten the joins. These cages are ideally sized 80cm x 60cm by 60cm (approximately 30 inches long x 24 inches high and wide) with a feeding verandah at

Above:
Heavily marked (reverse) Pied hen.

one end. They are economical to make, light in weight and are easily carried outside so that the birds can get some fresh air and sunlight. The weldmesh is much more suitable for climbing and can be painted black with water based paint to make the birds easier to see and the cage more attractive. The dimensions of the cage are well suited to a pair of cockatiels for good health and ease of maintenance. Trays can be made to keep the cage and the surrounding area clean.

Natural perches are much better for all birds in both cage and aviary situations. The varying natural dimensions create exercise for their feet and stripping bark seems to be an activity that keeps all cockatiels occupied for many hours. Of course, food and water dishes need to be placed away from the perches so that they do not become fouled and should also be placed where they can be easily accessed for cleaning and refilling.

Because pet cockatiels are usually housed inside, their owners may not consider aspects such as draught or cold. Many behavioural abnormalities and health problems are caused by unsuitable environmental conditions. For instance, many cockatiels are housed in the living areas of the home. When the human inhabitants require heat the room is heated for their comfort then the humans turn the heat off and crawl under doonas for the night, leaving their pet cockatiel to experience a rapid drop in temperature.

Cockatiels moult and breed in response to the change of season and the length of daylight hours. A pet cockatiel experiencing an unnatural range of temperatures and daylight hours will often develop feather problems and behavioural problems such as feather plucking as a result of this disruption. A simple solution is to keep your birds in a room that is not artificially heated during the day and move the birds to an unheated room when you turn the heat on in the evening.

It is also helpful to cover the birds in the evening if the room is draughty and lights should be turned off or the cage covered when it becomes dark outside. Cockatiels housed outside naturally roost from the onset of evening until dawn. Many people do not realise that their cockatiel is not genetically programmed to be up and active at midnight! Of course, for people who return home after dark, this is the only time they have to spend with their birds so in this situation it is best to extend their waking hours. The most important thing for their health and security is to be consistent.

All birds enjoy basking in the sun and this is especially true in winter. Sunlight is important for the production of Vitamin D3 and the absorption of calcium. While it is safe and very beneficial to hang your pet's cage in the sun in winter, the birds can die rapidly in full summer sun if left for too long. Ideally, the cage should hang where it receives morning sun only.

Yellow and green budgerigars are used as bait to trap and relocate troublesome raptors because hawks and other predator birds are able to spot them from a distance of up to five kilometres away. Your pet cockatiel of any colour would be just as effective as bait! Consider the hanging position of your cage carefully and try to provide some visual cover. If you are not going to be within hearing distance move the cage back inside. The distress call of a cockatiel is easy to recognise and quick action from the owner can usually rescue a pet from a potential predator.

Colour Breeding & Mutations

Colour Breeding

When obtaining new stock you may have to rely on the knowledge of the person supplying the birds and the hope that they understand genetics well enough to guarantee the true genetic background of the birds. Frequently, the latter does not apply, resulting in unsuitable pairings and many unexpected breeding results. The confused breeder may then pass incorrect information to the next purchaser based on the inaccurate results obtained.

Breeding for specific mutations of cockatiels involves three critical areas of administration apart from livestock management.

Above: Silver Spangle cock. Opposite page: Whiteface Silver cock juvenile.

Accurate Identification of Breeding Stock and Offspring

Breed only one pair per aviary to obtain accurate and guaranteed results.

Prior to the breeding season hens and cocks are housed separately. This is to prevent other cock birds mating with hens prior to being paired with genetically suitable mates. Hens can lay fertile eggs for up to two weeks after copulation. Many hens will commence excessive egg laying out of season when housed with cock birds and this will cause additional stress to the hens.

Hopefully, your initial stock will be close banded, but if not, they can be fitted with coloured plastic wrap around bands. The identification colour or band numbers should be recorded and their visual description noted. When their young are old enough they should also be banded and any additional genetic information should be added. For instance, if a lutino chick is unexpectedly hatched from a grey cock, you can note that the cock is split for lutino. In future, a more appropriate mate can then be chosen for that cock bird. You will also know that his male offspring will possibly carry forward this gene and the purchaser should be advised.

Chicks may be close banded anywhere from five days to two weeks of age, depending on how rapidly they are growing. Closed banding simply involves holding the three longest toes together pointing forward. The small, fourth toe is held back out of the way while the ring is slipped over the first three toes. Push the ring past the ball of the foot until it catches on the back toenail. The back toe is then gently levered forward through the ring by placing a toothpick between the leg and the back toe, in front of the ring. When chicks are banded at the correct time the ring will not have to be forced over the foot but there will not be an excessive amount of space either.

The chicks' toes are very flexible at this time but take all care to not harm the chick in any way. Banded chicks should be checked for several days following banding to ensure that the band has not fallen off or slipped up the leg.

We prefer to close band all of our chicks with encoded aluminium bands. Closed bands are available engraved with a multitude of different numbers and colours to identify the chicks. The bands we use have an internal diameter of 6 mm. Using a coloured plastic wrap around band on the other leg helps in identifying certain families when groups of birds are flying together.

People purchasing banded stock should be warned to ensure their aviaries are safe for banded birds. Closed bands can and will get caught on any small pieces of wire, twigs and hooks that protrude into your aviary. The result is gruesome if not fatal to the birds. Split bands are even more hazardous and are more difficult rather than less difficult to attach.

Accurate Record Keeping

All pairings, successful or otherwise, should be recorded in a breeding register. This will include details of the parents, the number of eggs laid, the date the first egg was laid, the date each chick was hatched, the band number of the chick and its genetic description. These registers not only help you to identify the birds you have bred but will help you to determine the success of individual pairs or specific lines of breeding. The register will also help you to know if the eggs are overdue in hatching and comments on other breeding aspects such as poor parenting skills or hatching difficulties.

An Understanding of Genetics

A modest understanding of genetics is by far the biggest hurdle most people face when breeding mutation birds, particularly when dealing with the pairing of multi-mutation birds. Whilst we can give people a list of what birds they can expect to breed from a pair that we supply, without understanding the principles involved they will often run into trouble with their next generation of young. Calculating the genetic outcome of a pair of multi-mutation birds, however, is really no more difficult than calculating a simple pairing if you understand the principles.

It is generally understood that the physical characteristics of all living organisms are passed from parent to offspring by the process of gene inheritance. Other than knowing that this does not refer to an article of clothing, most of us know little more than that about genetics! The basic principles of genetics are all one needs to understand cockatiel mutations.

As with humans and other animals, the individual characteristics of any bird are determined by the formation of the first cell in the reproductive process resulting from the combination of a male cell (sperm) and a female cell (ovum). Each of these cells, specific to reproduction, carries only half the genetic material found in the cells of most living organisms. Their combination results in a cell carrying a full complement of genetic instructions, half from the cock and half from the hen. This cell divides and multiplies as the embryo grows. Within the nucleus of each cell, this genetic information is carried on strands of DNA. These strands, referred to as chromosomes, are linked together in pairs, one from the hen and one from the cock. Situated along the length of the chromosomes are genes in corresponding positions forming pairs.

Genes determine our sex and physical appearance. When a pair of genes are identically matched, such as in the case of a child from blue eyed parents, the offspring will demonstrate that characteristic. However, if one parent had blue eyes and the other brown eyes, the brown gene is a dominant characteristic and will mask the recessive blue gene, resulting in a child with brown eyes.

FIG 1: Example of Autosomal Chromosome Pair

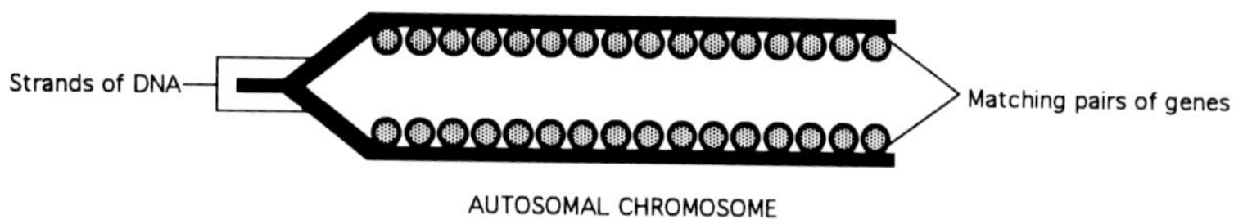

Autosomal Recessive

In most cases the wild colour of any species of bird is dominant to any other colour. Occasionally, the composition of a gene will be altered spontaneously, creating a mutant gene. These mutant genes are almost always recessive to the dominant normal gene and, unless the spontaneous mutation occurred on genes that determine sex, are referred to as autosomal recessive. They can be inherited for generations without becoming visible until two birds carrying the same mutant gene mate together. This is generally the result of random inbreeding in uncontrolled aviary situations.

Birds that have originated from wild type grey parents and are not carrying any mutant genes are referred to genetically as 'NN'. This is an abbreviation of the fact that the bird has received a 'N'-normal gene for colour from both parents.

FIG 2: Example of Autosomal Chromosome Pair Normal Colour - NN

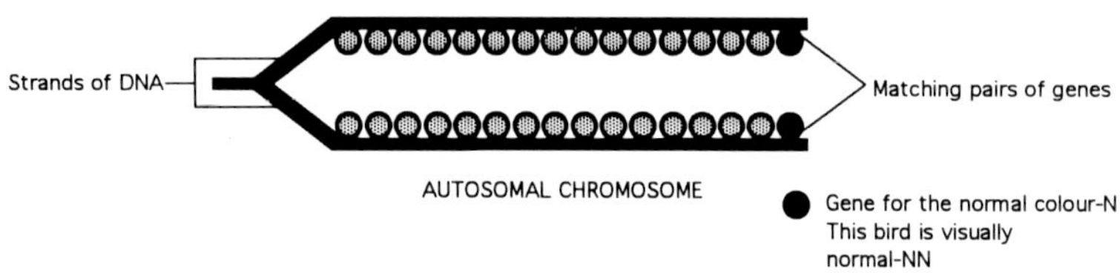

The pairing of two normal birds is charted as follows:

FIG 3: Normal Paired with Normal - NN x NN

HEN ↓ / COCK →	N	N
N	NN	NN
N	NN	NN

All offspring are visually and genetically normal- NN

The chart indicates that whichever way the chromosomes and the genes they are carrying link up, the resulting offspring will be normal, both in appearance and genetically. Birds carrying a mutant gene are referred to as splits and are abbreviated 'Nn'. The large 'N' refers to the normal gene and the small 'n' refers to the mutant gene.

FIG 4: Example for Visually Normal Bird split for Mutation Colour - Nn

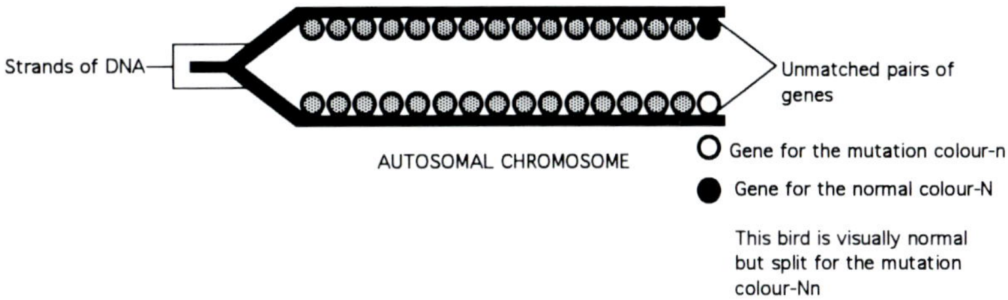

The pairing of two split birds is charted as follows:

FIG 5: Split x split - Nn x Nn

HEN ↓ / COCK →	N	n
N	NN	Nn
n	Nn	nn

25% of the offspring are visually and genetically normal- NN
50% are visually normal but split for the mutation colour-Nn
25% are visual mutations- nn

The chart indicates that the chromosomes can link up in four possible combinations. One possibility results in a bird that has not inherited the mutant gene at all and another is a bird that has inherited a mutant gene from both parents and therefore becomes visually different from the normal bird.

FIG 6: Example of Visual Mutation - nn

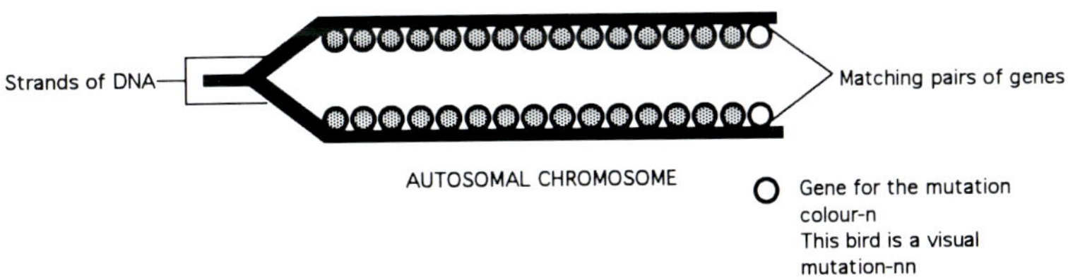

The other two possibilities involve birds that have inherited one mutant gene each. These birds are also splits but are visually normal because the normal gene dominates their appearance. It is not possible to tell which birds are carrying the mutant gene and therefore all offspring that are normal in appearance from this pairing are referred to as 'possible splits'. If a 'nn' visually mutated bird is mated to a 'NN' the pairing is charted as follows:

FIG 7: Normal x Visual Mutation - NN x nn

HEN ↓ / COCK →	N	N
n	Nn	Nn
n	Nn	Nn

All offspring are visually normal but split for the mutation colour- Nn

All birds will be visually normal but all birds must carry a mutant gene and are therefore definite splits.

If a 'nn' visually mutated bird is mated to a 'Nn' split bird, the pairing is charted as follows:

FIG 8: Mutation x split Mutation - nn x Nn

HEN ↓ / COCK →	n	n
N	Nn	Nn
n	nn	nn

50% of the offspring are visually normal but split for the mutation colour-Nn
50% are visual mutations- nn

In this case all birds have either inherited one mutant gene or two and are either visual mutations or definite splits.

If a 'nn' visually mutated bird is mated to another 'nn' mutated bird, the pairing is charted as follows:

FIG 9: Visual Mutation x Visual Mutation - nn x nn

HEN ↓ / COCK →	n	n
n	nn	nn
n	nn	nn

All offspring are visual mutations- nn

In this case all birds are visual mutations.

With autosomal mutations both hens and cocks can be split for a mutation colour. In the above charts you can change the sex of the split and the coloured bird - eg the combination of the split cock and a visual mutation hen can be changed to a split hen and a visual mutation cock, but the resulting offspring remain genetically the same. In cockatiels, the mutations of pied, pastel silver, fallow and whiteface are autosomal recessive mutations. Both hens and cocks can be split for these mutations. When charting the breeding of these birds, many people assign unrelated abbreviations to these mutations which causes the process to be more difficult for me to understand. To demonstrate the pairing of these mutations we use the following abbreviations:

Pd - pied F - fallow
S - silver Wf - whiteface Ss - silver spangle

Sample Pairings

FIG 10: Normal split Pied x Normal split Pied - N/Pd x Pd

HEN \ COCK	N	pd
N	NN	Npd
pd	Npd	pd pd

25% are visually and genetically normal-NN
50% of the offspring are visually normal but split for pied- N pd
25% are visual pieds-pd pd

FIG 11: Normal x Pied - N x Pd

HEN \ COCK	N	N
pd	Npd	Npd
pd	Npd	Npd

All offspring are visually normal but split for pied- N pd

FIG 12: Pied x Normal split Pied - Pd x N/Pd

HEN \ COCK	N	pd
pd	Npd	pd pd
pd	Npd	pd pd

50% of offspring are visual pieds- pd pd
50% are visually normal but split for pied- N pd

FIG 13: Pied x Pied - Pd x Pd

HEN \ COCK	pd	pd
pd	pd pd	pd pd
pd	pd pd	pd pd

All offspring are visual pieds- pd pd

Calculating Multi-Autosomal Mutations

This is done in exactly the same manner as the above charts. Take for example the pairing of a silver split pied cock with a pied split silver hen.

FIG 14: Firstly chart the pied with the split pied - Pd x N/Pd

HEN \ COCK	N	pd
pd	Npd	pd pd
pd	Npd	pd pd

50% of offspring are visual pieds- pd pd
50% are visually normal but split for pied- N pd

FIG 15: Then the Silver with the split Silver - S x N/S

HEN \ COCK	s	s
s	s s	s s
N	N s	N s

50% of offspring are visual silvers-s s
50% are visually normal but split for silver- N s

If you combine these two charts they will read as follows:

FIG 16: Silver split Pied x Pied split Silver - S/Pd x Pd/S

HEN ↓ / COCK →	N s	s pd
spd	N s spd	spd s pd
Npd	N s Npd	pd s pd

25%- N s s pd- silver split pied
25%- N s Npd- normal split pied and silver
25%-pd s pd- pied split silver
25%- s pd s pd-silver pied

You then simply read off the results - wherever a bird carries two matching symbols it is a visual mutation and where it carries only one it is a split.

Sex-Linked Recessive

One pair of chromosomes within a cell's nucleus differs from the others. This pair is responsible for determining sex. Males have a matched pair similar to their other chromosomes and like these, they carry a full complement of genes. This matching pair of male chromosomes is represented by the symbol 'XX'. Females do not have a matched pair of sex chromosomes. One of hers is identical to the male chromosome 'X', but the other is short and only able to carry a few genes concerned with reproduction. This short chromosome is represented by the symbol 'Y' and therefore, the female sex chromosome is represented by the symbols 'XY'. This differs from mammals, where the female carries a matched set of sex chromosomes and the male carries an unmatched set.

FIG 17: Sex Linked DNA

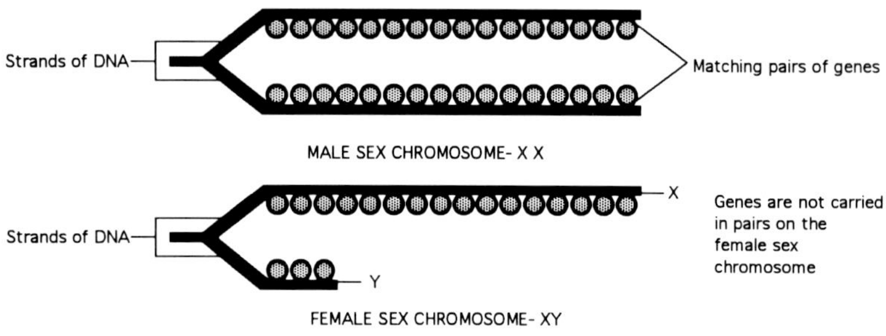

As mentioned earlier, when a new cell is formed by the union of sperm and ovum, each pair of new chromosomes originates from the combination of one donated by the cock and one by the hen. In all cases the cock donates an 'X' chromosome but the hen can donate either an 'X' or a 'Y'. If the newly formed cell receives an 'X' from the hen, it must develop into a cock - 'XX' but if it receives a 'Y' it will develop into a hen - 'XY'.

Therefore, it is the hen that determines the ultimate sex of her offspring. The union of male and female sex cells is charted as follows:

FIG 18: Sex Cells Only

		COCK X	COCK X
HEN	X	XX	XX
HEN	Y	XY	XY

50% of offspring are male-XX
50% of offspring are female- XY

The chart suggests that two out of every four chicks must be female, however, in reality we know that this is not always the case. A hen can produce ovum that predominantly carries the 'X' chromosome, resulting in a higher percentage of cocks in each clutch.

In some cases, certain mutant colour genes will appear on the 'X' sex chromosome. They do not appear on another chromosome and are therefore referred to as 'sex-linked' and are recessive to the dominant normal colour. Because males have a matched pair of 'X' chromosomes, they are able to carry the gene for normal colour opposite a mutant gene, therefore masking the effect. In this case the cock is visually normal but split for the sex- linked colour. The cock must carry a matched pair of mutation sex-linked genes before he will be the visual mutation colour.

In contrast, if the hen carries the same sex-linked mutant gene on her 'X' chromosome she will be the visual mutation colour with only one gene present. The short 'Y' chromosome is unable to carry the gene for normal colour opposite and therefore there is nothing to mask the effects of the mutant gene. For the same reason hens cannot be split for a sex-linked mutation colour. If the mutant gene is present on the 'X' chromosome, then it must show as a visible change in the hen's colour.

FIG 19: Sex Linked Mutation DNA

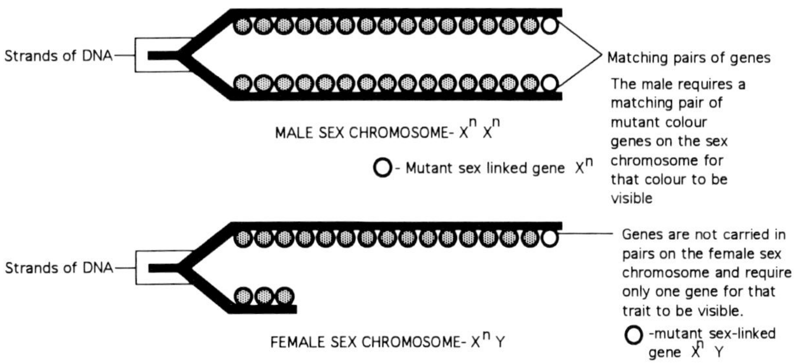

In cockatiels the mutations of lutino, cinnamon, pearl, platinum and yellowface are sex-linked. When charting the possible offspring from sex-linked mutations I use the following abbreviations:

C - cinnamon L - lutino Yf - yellowface
Pl - pearl Pt - platinum

Because a hen only needs to receive one gene to be visible for a sex-linked colour, it is important to include the symbols for the sex chromosomes, when charting the pairings of sex- linked birds. If not, it would be impossible to determine whether a bird displaying only one mutation symbol was a split cock or a visual hen.

A visual lutino cock bird is therefore assigned the symbols - $X^L X^L$

A split lutino cock bird is - $X^L X$

A visual lutino hen is - $X^L Y$

Sex-linked mutations are represented in superscript, above the X symbol. This immediately indicates that it is sex-linked and differentiates it from an autosomal recessive mutation. In charting sex-linked and multi-mutation pairings, I no longer use the symbol 'N' to represent the normal gene. This is not really necessary as any cocks or hens that do not have a matching pair of mutation symbols or hens that have no individual sex-linked symbols are always visually normal.

Sample Pairings

FIG 20: Split lutino cock x Normal hen - N/L x N

HEN ↓ / COCK →	X^L	X
X	$X X^L$	$X X$
Y	$X^L Y$	$X Y$

25% of offspring are split lutino cocks- $X X^L$
25% are normal cocks $X X$
25% are lutino hens $X^L Y$
25% are normal hens $X Y$

FIG 21: Lutino cock x Normal hen - L x N

HEN ↓ / COCK →	X^L	X^L
X	$X X^L$	$X X^L$
Y	$X^L Y$	$X^L Y$

50% of offspring are split lutino cocks- $X X^L$
50% of offspring are lutino hens $X^L Y$

FIG 22: Split Lutino cock x Lutino hen - N/L x L

HEN ↓ / COCK →	X^L	X
X^L	$X^L X^L$	$X^L X$
Y	$X^L Y$	$X Y$

25% of offspring arelutino cocks $X^L X^L$
25% of offspring are normal split lutino cocks $X^L X$
25% of offspring are lutino hens $X^L Y$
25% are normal hens- $X Y$

FIG 23: Lutino cock x Lutino hen - L x L

HEN \ COCK	X^L	X^L
X^L	$X^L X^L$	$X^L X^L$
Y	$X^L Y$	$X^L Y$

50% of offspring are lutino cocks $X^L X^L$
50% of offspring are lutino hens $X^L Y$

Calculating Sex-linked Mutations

Cock birds can be split for several sex-linked mutations or be visual for one mutation and split for up to four others, visual for two or three mutations and split for one, and so on. Hens can be visual for more than one sex-linked mutation such as cinnamon and pearl but cannot be split for sex-linked colours. In the case of a cock that is split for two sex-linked colours, the mutant genes can be carried on the same 'X' chromosome or he can carry one on each. When charting his potential offspring, two charts must be done in order to cover both possibilities.

FIG 24: Example of Normal cock split Lutino and Pearl x Normal hen - N/L/Pl x N

HEN \ COCK	X^L	X^{pl}
X	$X X^L$	$X X^{pl}$
Y	$X^L Y$	$X^{pl} Y$

$X X^L$ Normal split lutino cocks
$X X^{pl}$ Normal split pearl cocks
$X^L Y$ Lutino hens
X^{pl} Pearl hens

HEN \ COCK	X^{Lpl}	X
X	$X X^{Lpl}$	$X X$
Y	$X^{Lpl} Y$	$X Y$

$X^{Lpl} X$ Normal split lutino and pearl cocks
$X X$ Normal cocks
$X^{Lpl} Y$ Lutino pearl hens
XY Normal hens

As the charts indicate, there are eight different genetic combinations possible from this pairing, however all the cocks are visually normal and it is impossible to tell which are split to the sex-linked colours. Therefore, all the cocks are referred to as possible splits but the hens are either visual mutations or genetically and visually normal. If the cock was also split for cinnamon, four charts would need to be done to chart the cock bird's splits in the following combinations:

$X^c X^{Lpl}$
$X^{cL} X^{pl}$
$X^{cpl} X^L$
$X^{Lcpl} X$

Ideally, in the pairing of any two birds, the best possible combination is that of a visual mutation hen and a cock that is, at least, split for the same mutation. In this way all the offspring are visual mutations or definite splits. The same applies to multi-mutations. Following then, is a set of charts calculating the offspring of a multi-split cock and a multi- visual hen:

FIG 25: Example of Normal cock split Lutino, Cinnamon and Pearl x Lutino Cinnamon Pearl hen - N/L/C/Pl x L/C/Pl

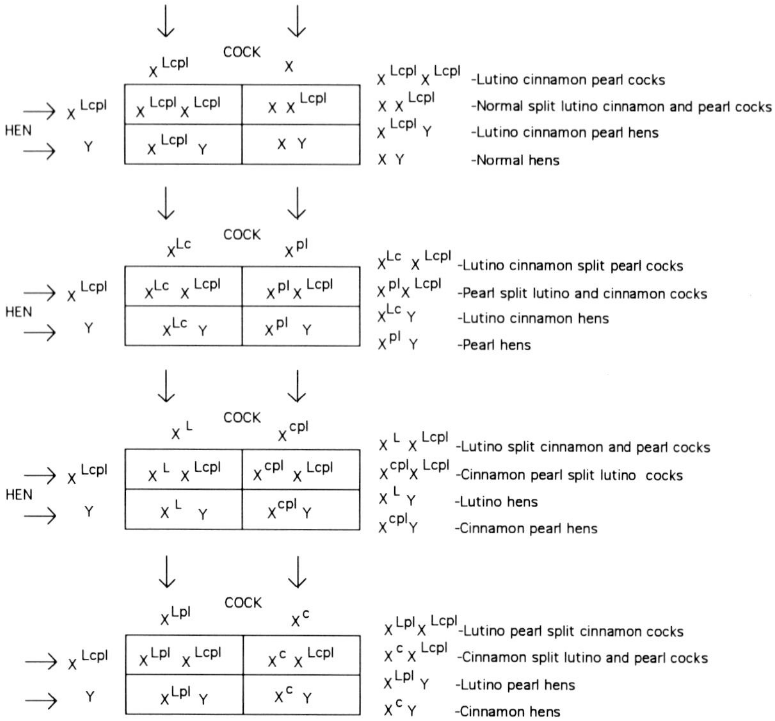

Calculating Combinations Between Sex-linked and Autosomal Mutations

Now we get to the tricky part! However, it's not really as bad as it might seem. In addition to being visual sex-linked colours or split for that colour in the case of cocks, a bird can also carry an autosomal mutation on another set of chromosomes. This will be visual in addition to the sex-linked colours if the bird has a matched pair of chromosomes or split if it only carries one mutant gene. An obvious example is pearl pied where the visual effects of both the autosomal recessive mutation pied and the sex-linked mutation pearl are visible at the same time. When calculating the breeding results of combinations between the two types of mutations, the principle is exactly the same.

All that is required is to chart the sex-linked and autosomal mutations on the same chart, doing as many charts as is required to cover the different possibilities.

FIG 26: Example of Normal split Pearl and Pied cock x Pearl hen - N/Pl/Pd x Pl

In this case I have introduced a single autosomal mutation gene to a cock carrying a single sex-linked gene. These can be inherited together or can be inherited separately and therefore two charts need to be done to cover these possibilities.

HEN \ COCK	X^{pl} pd	X
X^{pl}	X^{pl} pd X^{pl}	X X^{pl}
Y	X^{pl} pd Y	X Y

X^{pl} pd X^{pl} -Pearl split pied cocks
X X^{pl} -Normal split pearl cocks
X^{pl} pd Y -Pearl split pied hens
X Y -Normal hens

HEN \ COCK	X^{pl}	X pd
X^{pl}	X^{pl} X^{pl}	X pd X^{pl}
Y	X^{pl} Y	X pd Y

X^{pl} X^{pl} -Pearl cocks
X pd X^{pl} -Normal split pearl and pied cocks
X^{pl} Y -Pearl hens
X pd Y -Normal split pied hens

FIG 27: Normal split Pearl and Pied cock x Pearl split Pied hen - N/Pl/Pd x Pl/Pd

In this case I have introduced the same single autosomal gene to the hen. Again, these can be inherited together or can be inherited separately. In this case, four charts are now required to cover all the possibilities. Firstly chart the different combinations that can occur in the cock while the hen combination stays constant.

HEN \ COCK	X^{pl} pd	X
X^{pl} pd	X^{pl} pd X^{pl} pd	X X^{pl} pd
Y	X^{pl} pd Y	X Y

X^{pl} pd X^{pl} pd -Pearl pied cocks
X X^{pl} pd -Normal split pearl and pied cocks
X^{pl} pd Y -Pearl split pied hens
X Y -Normal hens

HEN \ COCK	X^{pl}	X pd
X^{pl} pd	X^{pl} X^{pl} pd	X pd X^{pl} pd
Y	X^{pl} Y	Xpd Y

X^{pl} X^{pl} pd -Pearl split pied cocks
Xpd X^{pl} pd -Pied split pearl cocks
X^{pl} Y -Pearl hens
X pd Y -Normal split pied hens

Then chart these same combinations with any other positions in which the hen's autosomal recessive genes can be arranged.

FIG 28:

HEN \ COCK	X^{pl} pd	X
X^{pl}	X^{pl} pd X^{pl}	X X^{pl}
Y pd	X^{pl} pd Y pd	X Y pd

X^{pl} pd X^{pl}	-Pearl split pied cocks
X X^{pl}	-Normal split pearl cocks
X^{pl} pd Y pd	-Pearl pied hens
X Y pd	-Normal split pied hens

HEN \ COCK	X^{pl}	X pd
X^{pl}	X^{pl} X^{pl}	X pd X^{pl}
Y pd	X^{pl} Y pd	X pd Y pd

X^{pl} X^{pl}	-Pearl cocks
X pd X^{pl}	-Normal split pearl and pied cocks
X^{pl} Y pd	-Pearl split pied hens
X pd Ypd	-Pied hens

In this case the pied has been separated from the hen's visual sex-linked gene and is now inherited by her female offspring. In the case of hens, sex-linked genes cannot alter position in hens because they must always ride on the 'X' gene. In this particular pairing both hen and cock are only split for the autosomal recessive gene 'pied'. As you can see by the charts, this results in pearl and visually normal birds, some that are split pied and some that are not, and also some visual pieds. As it is usually impossible to distinguish which offspring have inherited the gene, all non-visual pieds must be referred to as 'possible split pieds'.

Much more complicated pairings can be treated in the same way to supply you with accurate breeding results. Through experience, I am able to calculate the results of many pairings without resorting to pen and paper. For complex pairings I will always revert to this method in an effort to avoid missing any possibilities.

Introduction to Mutations

The appearance of a new mutation in a species is of interest to both the experienced breeder and the novice bird keeper alike.

Most mutations occur spontaneously in the wild and then specialist breeders can genetically engineer a mutation to its full potential. The preservation of normal cockatiels is an important part of breeding cockatiel mutations. We believe that high quality mutation cockatiels cannot be developed and maintained without also breeding high quality normal birds. This should be a natural and important part of every specialist breeders' breeding regime.

The cockatiel mutations that have been established in Australia are the pattern changes of pied and pearl, colour deletions of lutino and whiteface, melanin alterations of cinnamon and fallow, and grey melanin dilutions of pastel silver and platinum. The very beautiful silver spangle and yellowface mutations are currently being established, but are not readily available. As more people become involved in the breeding of cockatiel mutations an unlimited variety in colour and pattern will start to evolve.

Cockatiel mutations have been observed in the wild, and people have often referred to odd coloured cockatiels observed in wild flocks.

I have confirmed to my satisfaction that the genetic factors for lutino, pearl, pied, cinnamon, fallow, pastel silver and dark factors are in some birds derived from wild flocks. Dilute platinum is reportedly developed from wild caught birds. Strikingly different mutations such as lutino appearing in a wild situation would be unlikely to survive long because they would be such an obvious target to predators, either with feathers, claws or guns. Some of their grey brothers would carry this mutation factor.

George Smith, author of 'The Encyclopaedia of Cockatiels', estimates that at least 25% of normally coloured birds in the Australian bush carry a masked mutation factor of some type. It would be an interesting experiment if wildlife authorities would allow the controlled trapping of birds from more than one isolated area that could then be bred in a carefully documented breeding program.

The choice to breed mutations carries with it the responsibility to preserve the charming normal grey cockatiel as it appears in the wild. It is a myth that one needs to have wild breeding stock to improve any part of a responsible breeding program.

All of the birds illustrated in this book have been photographed by Diana Andersen in Western Australia. Most of the birds shown have been bred by the authors. Perth, Western Australia and Hobart, Tasmania have quite different climates. With thoughtful planning aviculturists from any part of the world can adapt management practices and avian accommodation to cooperate with Mother Nature and the extremes of her climate.

Mutation names and colour descriptions frequently differ between Australia and overseas areas such as Europe, the United States and South Africa. Cockatiels are freely traded between countries other than Australia so most breeding developments can be quickly and legally shared between international enthusiasts. Some colour forms may not be available to all countries but a common name may be used for another variety of similar appearance. This can lead to some understandable confusion.

The only `silver' bird now commonly recognised in the UK is the UK Silver, Dominant Silver, Dilute or Dominant Dilute Silver (all names for the same mutation).

One of the most frequent questions I am asked in Australia is about this UK Silver bird and the UK Platinum, which is the visual combination of the UK Dominant Silver and Whiteface. The book, 'Australian Cockatoos', by Stan Sindel and Robert Lynn is a gem of information about our cockatoos, including the smallest, cockatiels. However, it is important to know and remember that the colour photographs of the cockatiel mutations in 'Australian Cockatoos' are not Australian bred birds. Birds named platinum and silver in the UK are not identical to those of the same name in Australia, either in appearance or genetic inheritance.

Most of the overseas literature available states the UK Dominant Silver produces offspring in accordance with autosomal complete dominant breeding patterns. This mutation is said to be readily available because of the ease of breeding with a dominant factor.
That is: a double factor coloured bird of either sex paired to a grey bird will reproduce all single factor birds. A single factor bird paired with a normal bird will produce some single factor coloured offspring and normal appearing birds (grey). None of the grey birds should be split and therefore, WILL NOT carry the factor to future generations. Other literature refers to this interesting mutation as autosomal incomplete dominant. That is similar to the effect dark factors have on colouring. This is cumulative and is defined in single and double

factors but the visible expression is not as precise. The breeding results would not be as predictable as the first explanation.

The Australian breed of birds that look very similar to the UK birds have not matched the descriptions of autosomal complete dominant inheritance.

Many of the newer publications now feature the same or similar photographs, sometimes mis-captioned regarding sex or mutation identification. Comparing the various articles it is surprising how much difference in colour tones is apparent in different publications. No photo can substitute for seeing a particular bird or mutation variety 'in the feather'.

One breeder's 'primrose' or 'buttercup' yellow is another person's heavily suffused or deep yellow. I don't use the terms of buttercup, primrose or golden. Are the buttercup flowers that bloom in the spring in Washington State, USA a different colour than UK buttercups? Does Australia have a buttercup? Would a bird named Hibbertia pearl or pied conjure up a mental image of a lovely yellow for you?

We've always bred selectively for more yellow, choosing chicks with the brightest yellow down and the most noticeable yellow in their pre-juvenile feathers for future breeding. Yellow suffusion is so strong in some of our families that it may detract from some mutations, such as the pastel silver, and causes an olive green cast in some other varieties, including normal.

If Australian breeders used the Australian Government Colour Standard as a reference for colour description it would at least give us a base to build on when trying to describe a particular colour or pattern. These selective terms are of more use in marketing than breeding and are sometimes a good excuse for increased cost. Most of my descriptions and combination names imply genetic inheritance only.

Pied

One definition of pied is the alteration or disruption of the normal colouration in random areas as opposed to the pattern alteration of scalloping that is pearling. Pearling affects most of the body feathers. A bird can be pied with as little as one toenail not appearing the usual colour.

I stress the point of evaluating each individual bird because if one is discussing birds that normally have dark toenails such as normal, pearled, whiteface or yellowface the appearance of a toenail without colour should be a suspicious sign that the bird may carry forward genetically a pied factor. If one is defining a lutino, cinnamon, platinum or fallow colour change, all toenails would normally be without colour or light in colour already so the appearance of a dark toenail would be an indication that this bird could be carrying a pied factor.

One of my pied cocks has only a small stripe of dark colour on his beak. Another has a small patch of dark colour behind his crest that looks like a bald spot from a distance. These heavily pied birds are almost a clear pied, that is, with little or no visual indication that the bird is pied.

Clear and heavily pied birds are often mistaken for lutino or referred to as lutino pied. If you need to be sure whether a certain bird is pied or lutino look closely at its eyes with a strong light. A pied will not have red or ruby eyes, a lutino of any type will show red eyes, or sometimes a greyed eye with a lighter eye ring. Wing spots and tail barring would seldom, if ever, appear on a pied. Lutino pieds are as simple as pearl pieds to produce but only breeders with careful genetic records supported by closed banding and planned matings can produce a guaranteed lutino pied.

Pied factors seem to enhance the yellow in our birds, even in split or single factor pied which look quite normal otherwise but have a surprisingly strong yellow suffusion. Selective pairing can transfer the enhanced yellow from pied families into the other mutations without showing the pied.

The pattern disruption of pied is one of the most popular mutations. The lack of a regular, balanced pattern is part of the pied definition. However, selective breeding has proved that by consistently choosing breeding pairs that carry the desired markings, a high and quite predictable percentage of well marked pied birds will be bred. I prefer a pied bird to be about 75% yellow or white tones with the remaining 25% of its body the colour of choice. These birds are often referred to as reverse pied, a term I do not use. Cinnamon pied is a beautiful combination of colour and pattern, especially if the body markings are evenly balanced.

We breed specifically for clear faced pied. A clear face pied is simply a pied bird of either sex that shows no melanin based colour on its face. No brown, grey, dilute silver or platinum tones interfere with the otherwise typical cheeky cockatiel face. The presence of cheek patches is not disrupted by the pied factor and the orange can be large and bright in either sex.

The size and colour of cheek patches, depth of body colour, the presence or absence of under wing or under tail spots can be used as an indication of which sex the bird in question may be ... EXCEPT for pieds. The random disruption of normal feather patterns negates most of the traditional methods of attempting sex determination.

Patience and observation on the part of the breeder is one of the safest and most accurate way to determine the gender of pieds.

If you want a true pair of good pieds it would be wise to place a firm order with a breeder you trust and just wait. If you try to rock up and pick opposite sexes from a group of young birds lined up on a perch, feathers drawn in with suspicion as their bright little eyes watch you watching them you will have a 50% chance of obtaining a true pair. This is the same chance as the pelvic bone method on young birds, throwing coloured feathers over your shoulder or the method I really warm to ... "this bird bites harder and screams louder than the others so it must be a hen."

Combination Mutations

Pied combines well with normal grey and the colour changes of cinnamon, lutino, platinum, pastel silver, whiteface and yellowface. I have seen a beautiful fallow pied but the fallow birds I have would be too poor in strength, virility and size to breed with pied. The genetics of the silver spangle are not well enough understood to combine it with other mutations at this time.

Pied is inherited as an autosomal recessive factor. It is also thought to be partially dominant in that many birds with only one pied parent show a spot or some slight pied marking. For most of us it is enough

Above left: Heavily marked (reverse) Pied pair. Hen in foreground. Hens tend to be a deeper yellow.
Above right: Juvenile heavily marked (reverse) Pearl Pied cock.
Below: Heavily marked (reverse) Clear-faced Pied cock.

to know that both parents must carry the pied factor to produce a well- marked pied to admire in our aviaries. Both cocks and hens can be split or single factor pied and, although they may not show the pied factor obviously, they can pass on the capability to produce pieds to future generations.

A pied can be identified in a nest as soon as its crest pin feathers start to break through the skin at about seven days of age. The pin feather crest of pied chicks is bright yellow in all but a whiteface pied. Chicks will have the eye colour that is normal for the colour of the bird being bred. The pied factor only affects feather pattern, it does not alter eye colour so normal pieds will have dark eyes and cinnamon pieds will have plum eyes. Feet, legs and toenails are usually devoid of colour as pied does affect these areas but cinnamon, platinum, fallow and silver birds will normally have light coloured legs and toenails in addition to any changes pied may cause. You might find a dark coloured toe or beak stripe as a result of the random effect of pied.

The sex-linked pattern change of pearl was combined with the autosomal recessive pattern change of pied soon after the appearance of pearled birds in West Germany about 1967. The double pattern change is usually very attractive. This combination of pattern alterations can then be added to one or more of the colour changes for another whole series of interesting and pretty birds. All of the normal and mutation colours achieve their depth of colour potential when they are fully mature, about three years old. The more delicate colours such as platinum pied and lutino cinnamon pearl pied need this maturity to be fully appreciated.

Pied was one of the first mutations to be fully developed and is generally reported to have appeared in California about 1949.

From wild caught cockatiels I have bred youngsters that show pied markings such as spots of varying size, usually on the head and neck, mottled feet and toenails without colour. Neither parent showed any noticeable sign of pied. This particular pair bred 22 youngsters over a period of three years. Not one of these youngsters was pearled. However, when I bred a son with the most pied marks from this pair with a normal hen, they then produced one pearl hen per nest. Some of his sons proved to carry forward both the pied and pearl pattern genetic instructions. I still have this cock bird. I believe the pearling he produces in his daughters to be slightly different from the other pearl patterns we have. The genetic control of this family appears to be unstable in the inheritance of the normal cockatiel feather pattern. I do not backcross, that is breed daughter to father but as I breed the cocks to unrelated pure normal hens I will produce suitable pairs that may still surprise me with more changes. In early development I had hoped that the Australian pied might produce a significantly different pattern but this has not proved to be so.

Above: Lutino cock.
Right: Lutino cock and Whiteface split Pied hen.
Below: Lutino Pearl hen.

If our charming cockatiel had been in fashion as an interesting aviary bird these two mutations would have been developed long ago from birds that have always been, quite literally, in our own back yard.

Lutino

The lutino cockatiel cannot produce grey melanin anywhere on its body. The visible white, cream and yellow colouration so universally loved is the underlying yellow suffusion usually masked by grey melanin when the bird is visually normal grey. If one selectively breeds normal birds for more yellow suffusion the lutino birds bred from those families will be increasingly more yellow.

This sex linked colour mutation varies in colour from a pale, off-white to quite a bright yellow bird. Birds with the most yellow are usually combinations of lutino, pearl, and pied and have a strong yellow suffusion.

Lutino hens usually display more yellow and orange than cocks, when adult. All cock cockatiels gain a layer of dark colour when they are sexually mature. Because the lutino factor deletes grey melanin, the extra layer of colour appears like a shadow and could be described as mauve or pale lavender or 'dirty' wash over the cock's back, shoulders and wings. This overlay of colour highlights the white wing bar and it seems unusually white, but the effect is caused by the contrast in colours.

Long tail feathers and primary flights are usually a lighter shade of yellow than the body. The white wing bar is always retained, although it is not obvious and can be streaked with yellow in brighter specimens. The loss of grey unmasks the bright orange cheek patch and yellow crest in both sexes. Variation to size and colour of cheek patches on individual birds is normal and is not linked to the sex of the bird. Beak, cere, feet and toenails are off-white or pink toned which is the effect of underlying blood and veins.

Pairs can be arranged so the youngsters are identifiable by sex as soon as they hatch. Pairing a lutino cock with any hen other than lutino will produce red eyed lutino hens and dark eyed grey cocks split for lutino and whatever other genetic factors the hen may carry.

Newly hatched chicks have red eyes and yellow down. Lutinos have dark ruby eyes at maturity that are sometimes mistaken for black, and occasionally their eyes turn grey with a visible eye ring. This has no effect on their eyesight. Lutinos are affected by bright sunlight just as a person with light blue eyes is affected. Since birds can't wear sunglasses, providing overhead shade cloth or covered aviaries in areas with harsh sunlight is a comfort to these birds.

The lack of grey colour should be the main difference between good lutino birds and good normal birds. Well bred lutinos are as large, healthy, fertile and well conformed as any other quality cockatiel. They are not universally nervous and there is no reason why they should not have fully feathered heads. Undesirable traits, such as partially bald heads, have been bred into family lines by early inbreeding to increase numbers. Selective breeding could control and eventually eliminate this fault.

The first pair of cockatiels I bred was a lutino cock and a grey hen, that was in 1982. I still have one of the grey cocks split lutino from that first clutch and each year that I have breeding space for him he produces fine youngsters.

I have never bred lutino to lutino though I see no reason not to, provided both prospective parents have the qualities you require. I usually breed split mutation birds to visible mutations in alternate generations. With sex linked mutations I breed lutino, pearl, cinnamon or platinum cocks to pure normal hens and split cocks with mutation hens. I believe this method keeps more colour and size in my birds.

I choose lutino birds for future breeding by the depth of yellow in their down and the amount of pin feathers on their heads. I note these comments on their breeding records and then watch to see how they look when older than six months of age before I make a final choice. If a breeder is unwilling or unable to make nest inspections these details won't be noticed. After the youngsters have fledged, these qualities, which would improve the standard of next year's breeding, are hidden.

Quickly and correctly sexing lutino birds can be a challenge. If you are fortunate enough to look at a mature pair of lutino cockatiels for purchase there are many details to guide you about their gender. From a distance mature cock birds will look slimmer in their bodies and stand more upright on the perch. Hens will appear fuller in the body and when relaxed, sit lower on the perch.

Mature cocks will usually be less yellow than hens. If you can examine the birds closely, hens will show yellow barring on their under tail feathers and yellow spots on the underwing feathers, cocks will not have either. Cocks should have the coloured overlay on their shoulders and wings. This is a faint colour and varies with age and virility so if the lighting is not bright this could be missed.

Orange cheek patches can be large and colourful in either sex and are no guide to the sex of the bird. Typical gender behaviour is very accurate if they will cooperate while you are watching.

The pelvic bone method is not accurate unless your prospective hen is mature enough to lay eggs. If she is alarmed by being caught, turned over and fondled, she will tense her pelvic bones together and feel much more like a cock bird than a hen.

Combination Mutations

Lutino combined with the pearl mutation results in the typical cream and yellow body highlighted with darker yellow scallops where the pearl pattern would normally occur. If the pearl strain is heavily marked and strong yellow the resulting lutino pearl will be a more yellow bird. If the pearl factor is not heavily marked, the pearls might be only slightly visible on the lutino body.

When cock lutino pearls mature their pearls are no longer visual. Lutino pearls are sometimes called golden pearls which is not a precise name, although it is descriptive. Lutino pearl clearly describes their genetic status.

Lutino and pied can be combined effectively. I use two birds that are visibly pied or two that I can guarantee are definitely pied. One pair could be pied cock split lutino with a pied hen. All chicks would be pied and any lutinos would definitely be lutino pied hens. Another effective mating would be pied cock split lutino with a lutino pied hen. All youngsters would be pied and this pair would produce lutino pied cocks and hens.

Combining lutino, pearl and pied is even more beautiful and usually produces the most yellow birds of all, lutino pearl pied. A pearl pied split lutino cock mated with a pied hen would produce lutino pearl pied hens. As long as both parents are pied all offspring will be pied regardless of how many sex linked factors are included. When the yellowface mutation is combined with these multi-

Above: Lutino Pearl Pied hen.
Above right: Whiteface Lutino Cinnamon Juvenile.
Below: Lutino Cinnamon Pearl Pied hen..
Right: Juvenile Lutino Cinnamon Pearl.

mutations the result should be more golden.

Cockatiel breeders in Europe believed that cinnamon and lutino could not be combined visually. Lutino was thought to delete all melanin. Our breeding results have proved that the lutino effect removes grey melanin but does not remove brown melanin. Australian cinnamon is visible on the lutino body and provides another dimension of delicate colour. Lutino cinnamons have the typical lutino body of cream, white and yellow with primary flight feathers and tail feathers brushed with cinnamon colour. The cinnamon colour has all grey tones deleted from it so a warmer, brown tone remains. This colour increases in depth until the bird is about three years old.

Lutino cinnamon is even prettier when pearl is added. The pearls appear a deeper yellow on the white, cream and yellow lutino body and cinnamon colour (stripped of grey tones) edges the yellow pearls. A lutino cinnamon pearl combines two colour changes and a pattern change.

Adding pied to lutino cinnamon pearl will enhance yellow still

more. Pairing a cinnamon pied cock split pearl and lutino with a cinnamon pied hen will result in some lutino cinnamon pearl pied hens, a combination of two patterns and two colour changes. All youngsters will be at least cinnamon pied, some cinnamon pearl pied hens will also occur. If one is fortunate enough to have a cinnamon pearl pied cock split lutino and a cinnamon pearl pied hen all youngsters will be cinnamon pearl pied and any that are also lutino will be hens.

Breeding the two sex linked mutations of lutino and platinum together is inappropriate for reasons I will detail when describing platinum.

Lutino and whiteface produce a white bird that is very attractive. It will be called albino but to plan breeding results remember that it is simply a multi-mutation. Hens cannot be split lutino nor albino. Cocks cannot be split albino. Grey cocks can be split whiteface and lutino but those factors are carried on separate genes and will not always pass on to the offspring in the same fertilisation. Whiteface cocks split lutino paired with a split whiteface or visual whiteface hen will produce a percentage of whiteface lutino or albino hens. Whiteface cocks with lutino and cinnamon factors will produce whiteface lutino cinnamons or albino cinnamons when paired with whiteface or split whiteface hens.

Lutino combined with pastel silver is not effective because no grey melanin can show on its body. Any colour that might be seen is the brown tone that remains in the dilute pastel silver.

Lutino and silver spangle would be unsuitable for similar reasons.

Lutino and yellowface should produce an even more yellow bird.

The lutino mutation created a sensation when it occurred in Florida in 1958 and was quickly distributed all over the world from this initial breeding. In previous literature it has been referred to as albino. This was always incorrect since the bird retains the colourful orange cheek patch and varying shades of yellow.

Top: Lacewing Pearl cock-all pearling almost moulted out.
Above: Heavily marked Lacewing Pearl hen.
Right: Cinnamon Pearl Pied hen.

Pearl

Pearl is a feather pattern mutation that can be easily combined with any colour change. It is inherited in a sex-linked recessive mode. Cocks can carry forward this mutation unseen as a split bird but hens must be visibly pearled. A hen of any sex-linked mutation can never be split for the sex-linked factor.

Individual feathers over all or most of a pearled bird are affected by a lack of colour in a uniform pattern, very different from the large random areas of colour or lack of colour that characterise the feather pattern of pied. This type of patterning causes the feather to look scalloped. It can be coloured and edged with yellow tones or mostly yellow and edged with the body colour of grey or one or more of the mutation colours. An example of this would be a lutino cinnamon pearl where the lutino factor removes all grey traces and any cinnamon colour that remains trims yellow pearling across its back and shoulders. Flight and central tail feathers will show cinnamon also, especially when the bird in question is fully mature.

In the nest the pearl mutation cannot be identified until the chick is at pin feather stage. The pin feathers will look dotted or striped before the feathers break out of the feather casings. Its crest breaks through the skin a normal colour for the variety involved and its eyes are the colour that would be normal for the colour that is now pearled. For example, a cinnamon pearl would have plum eyes and yellow brown crest pin feathers, a lutino pearl has very red eyes and yellow crest pins, whiteface and normal pearls have dark eyes and dark pin feathers.

After fledging, legs and feet are a pinkish tone with a grey overlay of colour. Some families have quite pink feet but toenails are always dark grey in a normal grey pearl.

The pearling effect affects the tiny facial feathers so less body colour appears on the faces of hens. This allows the underlying yellow suffusion to be more visible and some hens have mostly yellow faces. This facial yellow is not as vivid as mature cocks. Hens also have yellow barring on their under tail feathers and yellow spots on the inside of their wings.

Both sexes can display equal amounts of pearling as juveniles. As cocks mature, their pearling is partially covered by the increase of melanin. If heavily pearled as a youngster a cock bird will retain traces of pearls on his shoulders and chest when he is fully mature. If he is lightly pearled, the increase of melanin as he approaches maturity more fully masks the markings. Cock cockatiels do not lose their pearls, their markings are simply covered over by the necessary melanin that indicates sexual maturity. When pearl cocks are aged or ill enough that they do not produce breeding hormones their pearls will become more visible again.

I have been told many times that an adult pearled cock looks identical to a normal grey cockatiel. I think careful observation would usually discover at least a regular shaded pattern of light and dark grey on the backs and shoulders of adult cocks.

We have found that many of the cocks who retain their pearls at maturity have not developed any interest in breeding. I theorise that they have never developed sexually because hens of different ages and experience simply ignore them and will even encourage an immature cock in preference.

Mature cock birds retain more of their visible pearling when combined with the pattern change of pied. I have no doubt that one day pearled cockatiels will be established in Australia that display their pearled pattern throughout their adult breeding life. Publications from overseas avicultural organisations suggest that selective breeding has 'fixed' the pearled pattern in some family lines.

I believe that several versions of pearling exist and have been unknowingly combined. During the breeding season of 1993-1994 I produced some pearled birds with pearling similar to fine pencil lines. I've bred pearls that have only been coloured on the feather shaft, gaining coloured edges to their feathers at maturity.

Combination Mutations

The pearled mutation can be easily combined with any mutations of colour or pattern. I recommend against breeding pearls into the spangled silver. This variety seems to combine a feather pattern and a colour change in the one mutation and mixing pearl into the new mutation would add to confusion. Pearl pied (two feather patterns), pearl cinnamon, pearl lutino, pearl pastel silver, pearl whiteface, pearl yellowface and pearl fallow are very attractive birds.

Pearled birds that display feathers with more yellow tones are often referred to as golden pearls. This refers to a heavy yellow suffusion that can affect any variation of cockatiel.

Pearls with less yellow and more of a white contrast to their body colour are occasionally called silver pearls. This is always incorrect unless it refers to a combination of the pastel silver and pearl, which is a beautiful bird at any time but even more so when combined with a heavy pearled pattern and a strong yellow suffusion.

Birds with heavy pearling affecting most of the body feathers are sometimes called lacewing. When does a pearled bird become a lacewing? This is another subjective term but it is also very descriptive as a heavily marked pearl has a delicate, lacy feather pattern. Lacewing pearl just seems to suit. An excellent specimen of a deep yellow heavily pearled bird may be worth a premium price but both buyer and seller should be aware that it is simply an attractive version of pearl.

The main thing most of the above names have in common is the possibility of making one bird sound more desirable to look at (and buy) than another. Only a personal viewing can determine for the buyer if a certain bird suits a desired mental image. Marketing terms are useful for sales but do little to imply genetic background. The unimaginative but genetically truthful names of lutino pearl, cinnamon pearl, platinum pearl, silver pearl or whiteface pearl should simply tell the prospective owner that the birds in question display a combination of a pattern change and a colour change. All of these mutation combinations should be equally well conformed, strong and fertile.

The pearled feather pattern often contributes better feather quality to other varieties when bred together. Even birds that do not display pearls, such as a normal hen bred from a split pearl father, may display a 'crowned' type of crest that is typical of pearled birds. I regularly use pearled family lines to improve head feathering, in any family.

Most sources believe that this mutation was first seen in 1967 in West Germany. It surely would have been available from our Australian bred cockatiels if anybody had been interested. In the chapter on pieds I include a description of pearled birds bred spontaneously from stock derived from wild birds.

Clockwise from top left:
1. Cinnamon hen
2. Cinnamon Pied cock.
3. Cinnamon Pearl hen
4. Cinnamon hen.
5. Pied cock and Cinnamon Pearl Pied hen.

Cinnamon

The cinnamon cockatiels now so readily available in Australia were first seen in the bush near Kalgoorlie, Western Australia. Jeanette Hickford obtained one of the second generation grey birds and established the long awaited colour of cinnamon by 1984. They have proved to be a typically strong, fertile sex linked recessive mutation with none of the problems often associated with new varieties. Cocks can be split to the cinnamon mutation but a hen can never be split to cinnamon

Clockwise from top left:
1 Cinnamon Pearl Pied hen.
2. Cinnamon Pied cock and Lutino Cinnamon Pearl hen.
3. Normal cock and Lutino Cinnamon Pearl Pied hen.
4. Normal cock and Whiteface Cinnamon hen.

or carry the factor unseen, the cinnamon must always be visible.

The information which appears in the Singil publication 'Australian Cockatoos' about the Western Australian cinnamon originating from a lutino hen and a normally coloured cock has, I think, been confused with the reputed origin of the Australian Dominant Silver (see silver spangle). The first recorded breeding reports of cinnamon coloured cockatiels were from Belgium in the late 1960's.

Cinnamon colouration in cockatiels is caused by the alteration of melanin granules that then produce a light brown or tan colour. This melanin alteration suppresses or dilutes grey tones that blend together to cause an overall colour effect of beige or fawn. The depth of brown toning varies between birds of the same family. Cinnamon colour is affected greatly by the age of the bird, its sex and physical condition. The birds are most likely to be at their peak appearance and colouration when about three years old after an annual moult. If you think your youngsters are nice, just wait until they grow up!

If the birds regularly receive a half day of harsh Australian sunshine some brown tones will be bleached out. Breeding stresses and incomplete nutrition will also affect the depth of colour. Marbling, a light and dark brown and cream shading, is caused by a diet deficiency or health impairment of some kind. It is not an inherited trait. Marbling is considered a fault if the bird is used for competitive showing.

Normal underlying yellow suffusion is more visible through the altered cinnamon melanin than is usually apparent on grey birds. This is noticeable on the chest and belly and any other area that would normally carry yellow in the feathering. The contrast between the cinnamon beige and a heavy yellow suffusion is very attractive, especially so when combined with the pattern change of pied.

Newly hatched cinnamons can be identified in the nest by obvious plum coloured eyes that change to normal dark brown at about two weeks of age. Crest feathers break through the skin a lemon colour. Cinnamon feet and legs appear a pale beige with light brown toenails.

Cocks and hens are identical as juveniles. Cinnamon melanin does not mask yellow as thoroughly as grey so more yellow is visible on the faces of hens. By at least four months of age young cocks will begin to show yellow streaking on their faces and they will practise a courting serenade as their voices change. Most young cocks (and some hens) will be attempting to sing at a much younger age but catching them in the act can be tricky.

Many times I've tiptoed around a wall to see who was singing only to find 20 pairs of bright young eyes watching me, all of them denying having uttered even a chirp in greeting. After being proved wrong in a few cases of sex determination I now don't trust any young bird to be a cock until I see him lift his shoulders to display. I have had many young hens with enough singing talent to fool anyone. They do not continue developing their song as much as cocks do, however.

At maturity cocks develop their typical yellow face and additional grey tones partially mask the brown and yellow shades of colour on the body. Sexual maturity causes a darker grey overlay on cock cockatiels. This effect occurs on cinnamon, fallow, pastel silver, lutino, platinum, spangle silver, pearl, whiteface, yellowface and normal cocks. Pied cocks do not show the effect as obviously, but their grey tones deepen and the yellow effect on their bodies is partially suppressed also. I follow a very basic guide. The more grey my cocks are the fertile I expect them to be.

Combination Mutations

Cinnamon colour factors combined with feather pattern changes of pearl and pied are very attractive. These combinations are some of the most sought after mutation birds. Pied seems to enhance yellow in an individual bird and this trait is even more attractive when combined with cinnamon.

It was previously accepted from overseas literature that the colour deletion of grey that causes lutino could not be combined with other mutation factors because lutino would completely overwhelm the other mutation effects. Jeanette Hickford proved this theory wrong in 1984 when she bred the "Three Sisters". Sister #1 was a cinnamon split pied, Sister #2 was lutino cinnamon pearl split pied and Sister #3 was a cinnamon pearl split pied. Jeanette wouldn't even tell me over the telephone about the lutino cinnamon because she was convinced that it couldn't happen. Lutino is now combined with cinnamon, pearl, pied, whiteface and yellowface very effectively. When the mutation factors of cinnamon and lutino appear together on the same bird the grey melanin is deleted from the cinnamon colour and the resulting brown tones are a much warmer colour.

Breeding with the Australian cinnamon and lutino has produced extremely beautiful combinations. Lutino cinnamon is much more striking when combined with the pattern changes of pearl and pied. Yellow pearled feathers are edged with cinnamon across the backs and shoulders. If the pied factor is added, it causes an increase in the depth of yellow and confines the attractive pearls to areas of cinnamon remaining on the body, usually on the shoulders and wings. Cinnamon pearl cocks will lose much of the pearled effect at maturity but the brightness of colour remains. Lutino cinnamon pearl, lutino cinnamon pied, and lutino cinnamon pearl pied are startlingly beautiful birds when seen at maturity.

Cinnamon and pastel silver colour dilutions are unsuitable to combine. The greyed effect of autosomal recessive pastel silver meets the cinnamon brown tones halfway. The cinnamon is greyed and the silver is slightly browned. The overall effect does not enhance either mutation.

Fallow combined with any colour change is unsuitable. We have had some birds appear that we think may be cinnamon fallow. Until further test breeding is conclusive I can only theorise that our cinnamon fallow birds look like a lutino cinnamon with very bright red eyes.

Cinnamon combined with platinum could alter the desirable brown tones of cinnamon with a greyed effect. Since both mutations are sex linked recessive it is possible that one of these mutation colour changes would be dominant over the other. I have been told of birds that may be this combination but I have not personally kept and test bred this combination, nor do I want to. These two mutations were bred together when the cinnamon colour first appeared. First generation offspring did not produce the new cinnamon colour and were consequently sold. All young cocks would have been capable of producing hens of both colours and a blended combination of both.

A photograph of a very attractive bird titled 'a dilute cinnamon hen' is in some of the newer publications. The genetic background of this bird is the UK dominant (dilute) silver bred with cinnamon.

Cinnamon combined with the newest sex linked mutation, yellowface, is very attractive. The yellowface mutation affects the cheek patch, changing the orange to gold. The normal yellow suffusion appears to be enhanced and the entire head of cock birds seems golden yellow. A cinnamon bird topped with a golden head will be very pretty.

Fallow

The fallow cockatiel is sometimes referred to as an advanced cinnamon that is inherited in an autosomal recessive mode. Both cocks and hens can be split and both parents must carry this mutation factor for any fallow offspring to be produced. It always has bright red eyes. An Australian fallow mutation appeared in the 1960's and several experienced aviculturists worked towards its development. I obtained some birds of this strain from Ron Rodda in South Australia. These birds were not bred with the fallows that appeared from the Western Australian cinnamon strain during 1984. There are several strains of fallow or autosomal recessive cinnamon in Australia. Overseas, a fallow mutation was reported first in Florida in the early 1970's.

Above: Red-eyed Fallow Pearl Pied hen. Right: Red-eyed Fallow Pearl Pied cock - juvenile.

Fallow is a delicately coloured mutation with tones of pale grey suffused with hints of brown, mainly on the backs of the birds. This mutation was understandably mistaken for the long awaited cinnamon. There are two colour phases to the Australian fallow and both cocks and hens can occur in either colour.

The hens of the silvery brown phase have to be described as a two-tone bird. Her face is dilute yellow with no grey masking effect and the same yellow tones continue down her chest but are more dilute. Viewed from the back she is an entirely different colour. Her back is mottled or shaded in grey tones with a hint of brown but is lighter than the Australian pastel silver birds.

Silvery brown phase cocks have more grey tones on their backs and their fronts are pale grey with less yellow than the hens. At least some of these grey tones are the result of the typical grey overlay of colour that male cockatiels develop. The other colour phase is very similar to a lutino cinnamon. Both sexes are alike. A fallow bird has bright red eyes while a lutino cinnamon, a more robust bird, will develop a darker, more ruby toned eye.

Most of our fallows have at least a partial bald spot on the backs of their heads and are a smaller bird than normal. Grey birds split fallow are a more typical cockatiel in size and constitution. Beak, legs and feet have virtually no pigment and appear an extremely pale tone of grey beige while toenails are pale beige.

Above:
Lutino Cinnamon Pearl hen.
Below:
Red-eyed Fallow Silver phase.

Some of my fallows were bred from the earliest cinnamon families which could not have been bred with other known fallow strains. My current stock all appeared from a normal grey cock bird split cinnamon and a cinnamon hen. Occasionally they would produce a chick with a brilliant red eye. These chicks often died even when serious attempts to hand raise them were made. At first I assumed they were lutino cinnamons but when some proved to be cocks I realised that I was working with something entirely different.

Fallows may have a 'lethal gene' involved in their mutation that could account for the high incidence of losses in the nest. The parents appear to neglect the fallow youngsters and the chicks often die. One theory I was able to discount was that the parents were neglecting the bright red eyed young and concentrating on the dark eyed chicks. I fostered two fallows under reliable parents who produced lutino cinnamon pearls, which have very bright red eyes, but the fallow youngsters were still ignored. When taken for hand raising many had plum coloured bodies as if they had a blood disorder. Newly hatched chicks have bright red eyes and when adult their eyes remain obviously red.

My attempts to encourage fallow birds of either sex or colour phase to breed have been consistently unsuccessful. The cock fallow, which looks very much like a lutino cinnamon, does not attract the attention of any hen. He is simply ignored. My choice was to use a selection of known, experienced grey hens who would normally encourage a cock bird to breed.

The hen, which is of the silvery brown colour phase, lays eggs periodically and sits, but no fertile eggs have been produced as all cocks seem to ignore her. She had a group of handsome, normal cocks from which to choose. I have never seen her mate with any cock bird. If the two fallows are in the same aviary they stay together, although they were not nest mates nor were they reared together. I have believed for a long time that these fallows have a different communication response. Perhaps they only understand each other. It is no surprise that this variation is not as well known as the other autosomal recessive mutations. It has not been as easy to breed and establish as the sex linked recessive mutation of cinnamon and, therefore, it is not as available. There is much developmental work to be done with this mutation.

Combination Mutations

Fallow has been combined with mutations of both colour and feather pattern to produce unusual specimens of fallow pied, fallow pearl and silver fallow. Any combinations must have red eyes. With the current understanding or, rather, lack of understanding of breeding fallow cockatiels I would not deliberately combine fallows with any colour mutation.

Combining fallow with feather pattern changes has been attractive. The addition of the pearl factor often improves feather quality in most cockatiels. Some strong, apparently healthy and reasonably large fallows appeared from sex linked recessive cinnamon families during the 1993 breeding season. The birds are combined with pearl and pied.

When we, as aviculturists, develop the fallow mutation into a strong, fertile and good sized bird I would like to see how a pastel silver fallow bird would look. The silver fallow I have viewed was a beautiful bird. It had a pale silver body and red eyes and was sitting on a perch next to a whiteface hen. I didn't even notice the whiteface because the silver fallow was such a lovely bird!

At that time there was some controversy in cockatiel breeding circles because the silver fallow was considered a blended mutation and not a mutation in its own right. It was the result of breeding a silver bird and a red eyed fallow. I failed to obtain any information of the type of silver bird used and have never seen descriptions in any literature of this silver.

Certainly the appreciation of a 'blended' colour has improved when one considers the demand for the albino, a blend of whiteface and lutino.

Silver

The Australian Silver mutation is a dilute silvery grey bird that inherits its colour in an autosomal recessive mode. Cocks and hens can be split to this mutation and both parents must carry the mutation, even if not visible or suspected, for a chick to show the pastel colour.

This mutation first appeared around 1982 in western Australia. it was hoped this was the long awaited cinnamon but outcrossing and test breeding in my aviaries quickly proved that it was not a sex-linked recessive factor. Photographs of the first nest I bred that produced a 'Silver' bird show a lutino chick, a grey chick and a brown chick. the brown tones are very obvious but the bird matured to be quite pale grey, especially on its chest.

Pastel silver is a light grey colour with the hens usually appearing slightly darker than the cocks. hens change little in depth of colour from their juvenile stage to maturity. Cocks are usually lighter in colour than hens at fledging and will gain a few shades of darker grey on their backs when mature. The fledging colour is a guide to early sexing of this variety. Melanin overlay caused by sexual maturity produces the darkening effect. This is similar to the loss of pearling in pearled cock birds. The chest and belly of cock birds remain as light as the juvenile bird. I still have the first silver cock bred and he is as lightly coloured from the front as the first photographs show.

The birds' feet are lighter than normal grey birds and toenails are a light grey-brown tone. Even on darker silver birds the toenails will define that the bird is a pastel silver. Eyes are marginally lighter under the skin at hatching than a normal grey chick and turn dark brown within 10 days of age. Hens often have a speckled chest but I have never noticed a cock bird with this characteristic. This dilute variation does not inherit single and double factors to affect its expression of pastel silver. The darker birds may be affected by dark factors. Heavy yellow suffusion causes the bird to look olive green. This is one mutation that is usually more attractive with less, rather than more, yellow. However, a pastel silver bird with heavy pearling and strong yellow suffusion is very beautiful.

There is a wide variation in the depth of pastel silver colour in cock birds. Darker individuals can produce lighter coloured youngsters. Selective breeding for pale colouration and less yellow is producing birds that are lighter in colour each generation. This is a tricky selection for me as I have happily chosen young birds with the most visible yellow since 1982.

Traditionally, silver birds were silvery or steel grey in body colour and had red eyes. it is now accepted that silver comes in many shades of diluted grey. Brown tones can be seen in the feathers in varying amounts which has led to the autosomal recessive colour being mistaken for cinnamon. I look forward to seeing the classic *'Red eyed Silver'* someday.

There are several strains of uniformly dilute or pastel 'silver' birds now being developed in Australia. all of these silver (dilute) grey birds have so far been an autosomal recessive mutation. They should all breed equally as well when carefully developed. More importantly, their conformation, size and virility should be equal to the sturdy, normal cockatiel.

Silver Cockatiels were reported in Europe in the 1960's and then later in New Zealand. Many references can be found that state early strains suffered from lethal factors and blindness. I was fortunate to talk to Dr. G. Th. F. Kaal of Holland, a speaker at the 1991 Avicultural Federation of Australia convention in Hobart. Although I had never seen in print that he was involved with these 'blind' silvers he informed me that they were his birds. The full story was that only a few birds had problems and after the first generations the red eyed silver cockatiels were quite normal in eyesight and health.

I observed red eyed silver and fallow birds in the US in 1984 and at that time they were as strong and fertile as the normal grey cockatiels. The combination of two autosomal recessive mutations was successful and the resulting silver fallows are available in the United States. The cockatiel mutation poster from Holland 'Valkparkieten' features a dilute silvery grey bird that is captioned Pastel Silver. From the photograph the bird looks to be uniformly lighter grey than normal. The autosomal recessive pastel silver bird we breed here is much lighter on the front of the bird than on its back.

Combination Mutations

Pastel silver pearl is attractive, especially so when the pearling is heavy and combined with a strong yellow suffusion. in my breeding experience the pattern alteration of pied seems to enhance yellow and I've not yet bred a pastel silver pied that has satisfied my image of a silver pied. I have been told of other breeders producing fine pastel silver pieds from our families. We have the genetics paired up so maybe this year is the year for us to do so.

Combining the autosomal recessive silver with sex linked cinnamon is not attractive. The resulting birds are an indistinct colour, neither very cinnamon nor very silver. Predictions were that the combination of the two mutations would produce a 'cream'. This has not occurred.

The lutino mutation deletes grey melanin and lutino silver birds may show a slight edging of darker colour along the flight feathers at maturity but no silver colour is obvious. If any colour is noticeable it is the slight cinnamon tones that remain in the pastel silver. Lutino does not delete the cinnamon melanin.

Top right: Silver cock.
Top left: Whiteface Silver, Whiteface Silver Pearl and Lutino Whiteface- (Albino).
Right: Silver Pearl Pied cocks (juvenile)

Cockatiel colour variations increase in richness until the birds are at least three years old. The more delicate colour combinations may not be noticeable in juvenile birds.

Combining the pastel silver with platinum might cause a lighter colour effect. since pastel silver is inherited as autosomal recessive and platinum as sex linked recessive a cumulative effect could occur without a chromosomal conflict about which mutation, if any, will dominate. However, because of the confusion that currently exists with the platinum genetics I would be very cautious about dong so. Until the lutino and cinnamon mutations are thoroughly bred out of the platinum variation an autosomal recessive factor bred into this line would only make definite colour breeding more difficult.

Above: Platinum Pearl hen. Below: Platinum Pearl cock. Pearls have moulted out with maturity.

Whiteface silver is an exceptionally attractive bird. This double autosomal recessive combined mutation had no dominance problems in its expression. All yellow and brown tones remaining in the pastel silver are removed and the birds are a pastel version of the normal grey whiteface. Even young hens have a very pale face with little or no pastel grey showing on their faces although they do not have the brilliant white face mask the adult cock develops. Whiteface silver pearl is exactly as expected and is very attractive in the more heavily marked birds. Whiteface silver pied should give me a bird to satisfy my mental image because all the yellow suffusion will be gone. We should see this combination and Whiteface silver pearl pied in next year's breeding.

Australian aviculturists have a patterned dilute grey mutation available which has been commonly called Dominant Silver because of the apparent similarity to photos of the UK Dominant Dilute Silver, now usually called Silver in recent literature. I now refer to this Australian mutation as UFO (Undefined Flying Object) silver spangle. For several reasons this variation of dilute has been unreliable to breed. Out test breeding is well advanced now after starting over with fresh out crossing and controlled records in 1991. Our breeding results to date indicate that his attractive mutation is not dominant in inheritance.

Within two years we could have a whiteface silver spangle that may look like the platinum birds often seen in photos from the UK. I intend to use a name that will reflect the genetic background of this combination mutation. A genetically descriptive name should be easy to implement because, at the time of writing, the names of platinum and silver have been attached to two entirely different mutations in Australia.

Platinum

The name platinum was selected by the Australian National Cockatiel Society to describe a sex linked recessive bird of extreme dilution. Only cocks can be split to this mutation and carry forward the genetic directions unseen. Hens must always be visibly platinum regardless of any pattern that may be combined with the colour.

This mutation may be the most often misrepresented variety that we breed in Australia today. It has been inadvertently and deliberately advertised, sold and purchased as Cinnamon, Silver, Black-eyed White, Lavender wing, Cafe au lait, Lutino, Albino and, undoubtedly, a few other names. I've never seen a photograph or description from overseas of a cockatiel mutation that resembles this variation. This interesting variety may not yet be available to overseas breeders.

It is a difficult colour change to describe. One guide to identification is its eye. Eyes of newly hatched chicks vary between bright red (identical to lutino chicks) and plum (identical to cinnamon chicks). By one week of age the youngster's eyes usually look dark. Many birds of this mutation acquire a visible eye ring when mature, giving the appearance of a two toned grey eye. However, not all individuals acquire this characteristic. Infant birds are identifiable by their eye colour and their pin feather crests, which break through the skin before other feathers and are very light in colour.

The platinum should be a pale smoky grey colour overall. The normal underlying yellow suffusion is evident over most of the body and yellow appearing on the face and crest is as bright as any typical cockatiel. The smoky grey colouring is more obvious on the long tail feathers and primary flight feathers, as is expected from most colour forms. The typical yellow face and orange cheek patches differs only slightly between the sexes. Feet, toenails and legs are a pale beige tone.

White described on a lutino is brighter and clearer than the smoke toned white in this mutation. These are all very subjective words. 'Smoky' colouring may be different in my imagination than yours. Until an independent and official colour standard is agreed upon and used by all breeders for reference, colour descriptions will generally be inadequate. Mere words cannot substitute for personal observation of mature birds in good condition and feather.

Robyn Ashton of Brisbane, Queensland, who breeds fine examples of the platinum, stresses that this mutation should be considered a solid coloured bird of pale smoky grey colour. The colour is spread on the bird the same as a normal or cinnamon. She also notes that cocks tend to become darker as they mature. Her breeding results have been in accordance with typical sex linked recessive genetics.

Part of the difficulty in identifying this mutation is the fact that platinum birds have been bred with lutino and cinnamon. Whichever way these mutations were mated the resulting grey males carried the genetic instructions to produce youngsters of each colour and combinations of one, two or even all three colour changes. Unidentified results of this genetic combination have been distributed within the bird keeping community. Unaware or uninformed new owners then bred a surprising variety of lutino, platinum and cinnamon combinations. The surprising part was only because the light coloured birds were not known to carry all the genetics. The results might have been fairly easy to explain if all the possible genetic factors had been charted.

How can a lutino platinum, cinnamon platinum or a lutino cinnamon platinum be identified? At first it appears to be a contradiction in terms. But, now we know that lutino does not delete the melanin that causes brown tones. A grey cock bred from a platinum parent and either a lutino or cinnamon partner would be a simple double split combination, the same type of pairing that produces lutino pearl or cinnamon pearl.

However, some combinations are not as effective as others when they are produced. When paired with any hen a grey cock double split for platinum and lutino would produce varying percentages of platinum hens, lutino hens and lutino platinum hens. Some of the latter would be hens that don't look quite lutino but don't look quite platinum either. Grey cocks split for platinum and cinnamon would produce platinum hens, cinnamon hens and cinnamon platinum hens from a similar mating.

Lutino platinum birds would have no grey colour and any slight brown tones occurring in platinum would still be visible. A platinum cinnamon would be an indistinct blended tone, neither fawn brown nor dilute grey and difficult to identify without test breeding.

If the breeder obtained a visual platinum cock that was also (unknown to the breeder) split to lutino and/or cinnamon all young hens from any mating would be platinum and some would appear visually platinum lutino, platinum cinnamon or platinum lutino cinnamon. These young hens would look very different from each other. This type of breeding has led to some unusual theories about its genetics.

The Australian National Cockatiel Society is overseeing some test breeding of the dilute platinum mutation. The platinum mutation may prove to combine alleles where at times one type of colour could dominate over another carried on the same gene.

I test bred the platinum mutation outcrossing to my own normal birds. I paired a grey cock allegedly split for the undetermined genetic factor with one of my normal grey hens. Subsequent breeding produced dilute platinum hens, pearl hens, platinum pearl hens, grey hens and grey cocks. Some of these second generation cocks proved in further test breeding to be normal grey and not split for platinum or pearl. Others produced either platinum or pearl hens or combinations. After several years I was satisfied that the extreme dilute factor I was test breeding was inherited as a straightforward sex linked recessive. I could see no purpose in continuing to test breed this mutation with lutino or cinnamon after analysing my breeding results.

Combination Mutations

The delicate platinum colour combines very effectively with pattern changes. Platinum pearl is very pretty, especially when heavily marked pearls are used in the combination. Platinum pied causes the yellow suffusion to be enhanced and provides a pleasant contrast to the random appearance of smoky grey colour. Platinum pearl pied is a combination of two feather patterns with the dilute colour. The pearling is confined to the remaining areas of platinum colour, usually shoulders and wings and is very attractive.

When platinum and whiteface are combined, the offspring should be extraordinarily pale silver with the stunning white face. There will be little difference in appearance between the sexes.

Platinum yellowface birds will display a smoky grey body and a golden head. Hens should be almost as colourful as cock birds.

The platinum mutation cockatiels are typical strong, healthy birds with no inherent faults such as baldness and low fertility. They are attractive birds with all the charm and personality of any cockatiel. This interesting variety is readily available. To avoid the confusion described here, it is worthwhile searching for breeders who can guarantee the genetics of their birds.

Above: Silver Spangle cock.
Below: Silver Pearl hen.

Silver Spangle

I refer to silver spangle in the following text, possibly in more detail than you will enjoy or ever want to know. The description of silver is usually applied to a dilute grey autosomal recessive mutation. The additional description of spangle will, I hope, evoke an image similar to the appearance of the birds in question. Choosing a descriptive name without additional confusion and marketing influence was my goal.

On the basis of our breeding results to date we no longer suspect that the mutation commonly referred to as dominant silver in Australia could be inherited in a dominant mode. This mutation has reproduced itself in accordance with autosomal recessive expectations and seems to combine a colour and pattern change. We may still prove that we are breeding with single and double factors in the expression of this beautiful mutation, similar to the spangled budgerigar.

The birds are very attractive. Close inspection reveals the striated, shaded appearance is caused by individual feather barbs growing from the shaft in light and dark shades. The entire body is affected with the head less shaded.

The dilution affects the grey and yellow that normally appear on the body. If the bird is a light silver tone, its yellow is also light although the underlying pale yellow suffusion may be obvious throughout its body. Silver shading to some degree is always apparent over the shoulders and down the back and wings.

Most mutations, even lutinos, retain the distinctive white wing bar that is unique to the wild type cockatiel. Previously, only the random

Left: Back view of a Silver Spangle.
Above: Silver Spangle

disruption of colour caused by the pied mutation has affected the placement of the wing bar. The shaded colouration of our spangled silver intrudes into this area. Heavily marked individuals have no distinct white wing bar. All have the shaded colouration blending thoroughly across the full wing. Usually shoulders are a bit darker, but still shaded or spangled. To achieve the distinctly silvery shaded look, the grey melanin is both partially deleted and diluted in areas that are normally grey and shaded grey melanin is distributed into areas that are normally white.

Eyes are dark brown at hatching and as adult birds. Feet and toenails are dark grey like the wild type greys. Until the 1993-94 breeding season we had not been able to identify the silver spangle chicks until the feathers were well erupted from their casings. However, one of the birds hatched during February 1994 was noticeably pale in the nest and did prove to be the lightest silver spangle that I have yet bred. Its white wing bar is obscured totally by the striated intrusion of the light and dark shades. Feet on this young cock bird were also lighter.

To continue working towards this genetic mystery, we consider that this bird could be double factor. If this cock produces all silver spangle birds with a normal hen or some exceptionally pale youngsters when paired with another silver spangle, I will feel more secure with the theory that it has a single and double mutation factor. Another possibility is that it may be a partially dominant or an incomplete dominant factor, similar to single and double dark factors. Perhaps two mutations are occurring together and are not visible singly.

This mutant bird appeared in Western Australia in the early 1980's. I first observed some of these birds in 1983 and obtained some in 1984. By 1990 other breeders and I had achieved little progress in the development of this strain. I had produced only one silvery bird and the pairs were indifferent about breeding even when provided the opportunity to choose a partner from a flock situation. Breeding records were obtained from the original breeder and compared with my own experiences. No controlled line breeding or out crossing had been done since 1981. Birds were not close banded and family records did not exist.

This first silvery bird in this mutation is said to have appeared from the mating of a grey cock and a lutino hen. Subsequent generations have produced some apparent whiteface and albino. This line is unrelated to whiteface strains that have appeared elsewhere in Australia.

During 1991, shortly before I moved birds and household to Tasmania, I found two newly hatched, plump and apparently red eyed chicks in a nest from a visibly coloured cock and a grey hen from the 'family". Closer inspection confirmed that the chicks were not red eyed but had no eyes at all! These chicks were the catalyst for serious review and reorganisation of our breeding program for the, as yet, undefined but very beautiful mutation.

The successful establishment of an attractive, healthy mutation is not a casual task. Undesirable or lethal traits may appear or be intensified and cause poor growth or unexplained mortality. Altered gonads and unusual internal organs are just some of the unwanted factors that are possible and should be considered probable when working towards developing a mutation into a strong, healthy bird.

One of the first traits to suffer with indiscriminate inbreeding or very close line breeding is fertility. Reviewing the original records confirmed there was no way to verify how closely related the birds were that I had been attempting to breed. The disruption caused by moving across country was the perfect opportunity to pair the UFO silver cocks with personally bred unrelated normal hens.

The breeding records of 1991 show forty-five offspring were produced. None showed the characteristic silvery, spangled, shaded markings. The simple explanation of an autosomal dominant mutation certainly indicates that about 50% of chicks from a pairing of a dominant mutation bird with a normal bird should be visibly marked. A huge majority of the chicks were cocks but a few precious hens were obtained. Anecdotal evidence indicates that it is not unusual for new autosomal recessive mutations to breed far more cocks than hens in the early years of development.

The next generation required the mating of silver cocks with hens bred from one of the other silver cocks. No daughters were bred back to their fathers. Two pairs bred and both produced silver spangled birds. Finally we produced a silver spangle hen. Unfortunately, this hen had a crop disorder and will not be used for breeding. The unusual problem may be genetically inherited.

The second pair produced fourteen youngsters. At least seven of the chicks were visibly marked. Three birds display only slight markings. Four of the young birds showed a clear visible expression of the desired silvery, shaded effect. Two of these, both cocks, are extremely light in colour with the shaded silvery colour interference intruding through and obscuring the white wing bar. Two of the youngsters are HENS! These young hens are not as spangled nor as light in colour as the cocks.

The breeding results from the first cross in the reorganised breeding program points to an autosomal recessive inheritance for this beautiful mutation. The second generation results are exactly the same percentage that a visible and a split autosomal recessive mutation would produce. For example, breeding a whiteface to a split whiteface would result in 50% whiteface offspring.

This mutation has always been slow to mature in colour and often birds show slight markings after their one year moult that have not been noticed as a juvenile. All the youngsters will be kept until the second year - just in case!

One of the pale young cocks will be paired to an unrelated genuine normal grey hen. I won't be able to resist the temptation to breed one of the young hens to a silver spangle cock. If there is a double and single factor influencing the expression of this mutation, that pairing should prove it.

The controlled and carefully documented breeding program for silver requires regular out crossing to the best possible pure normal birds. This procedure should help ensure that all the reliable qualities of fertility and strength typical to cockatiels are fully developed. My personal preference is to breed a mutation bird of any type to a split or normal every other generation. I believe this maximises the best qualities available. Of course, selection of the best stock in all the normal birds must be exercised with each pairing. Effective selective breeding cannot be done without flock record management. Closed banding is absolutely necessary.

This is a mutation that I would not yet combine with other variations. To put the current breeding unreliability and possible genetic deformities into other families would be irresponsible. Many questions of development remain, such as, can the colour and pattern be separated when combining different characteristics? Could the melanin grey be altered to cinnamon melanin and the pattern remain? It's obvious that the genetic inheritance is not completely understood, at least by me!

Lutino has already been bred with this mutation resulting in lutino hens that may also be silver spangle. Since the lutino factor deletes grey melanin no obvious proof of the feather pattern disruption remains. We do have some lutino hens that seem to have an interrupted pattern of yellow barring on their under tail feathers but, as yet, no proof that they are also silver spangle.

One comfort about this combination is that these lutino hens all have excellently feathered heads. A worry is that if these lutinos are used to improve lutino families a percentage of all youngsters will genetically pass on the silver spangle. Future breeding can gradually remove lutino from the silver spangle families.

In theory, future combinations might be as follows.

Combination Mutations

Combining silver spangle with the pearl feather pattern might detract from the unique feather pattern change that this beautiful mutation displays.

Pied silver spangle should confine the shaded silver effect to areas that would appear grey on the pied bird.

The prospect of combining whiteface with our silver spangle is exciting. All of the orange and yellow tones in the silver spangle birds would be deleted and it should be a very beautiful silvery bird. This combination could look like the UK Platinum. That name is claimed by the sex linked platinum in Australia so our new multi-mutation could have a genetically descriptive name, such as

whiteface silver spangle!

This beautiful silver spangle is a mutation cockatiel that presents breeders with a true challenge.

Whiteface

The whiteface mutation is a result of a colour deletion that has a spectacular effect on all variations of cockatiel. Whiteface removes all yellow and related tones of orange or red from the entire body. This is the exact opposite of lutino, which prevents all grey melanin production on the bird. One could photograph a normal grey whiteface mutation with black and white film and the effect would be no different than using coloured film, except for the background.

Whiteface is inherited in an autosomal recessive mode. Both parents must carry the mutation factor to produce a visually whiteface youngster. Hens and cocks can be split and appear to be normal grey. A split whiteface bird will not show any white spots as a result of the whiteface factor. Usually a bird displaying a spot without colour is carrying forward a pied factor.

Above: Whiteface Pearl hen.
Below: Whiteface Cinnamon Pearl hen.

Whiteface cocks have a grey body which is slightly shaded light and dark as are all mature cocks. They develop a brilliant white face and neck when mature, black tail feathers and a white crest shading into deep charcoal. No yellow suffusion is possible anywhere on the body. The most surprising observation, when observing whiteface cocks for the first time, is the absence of their coloured cheek patch. The cere, feet and toenails are also charcoal coloured. Eyes are dark brown.

When whiteface birds were first developed they were named charcoal, a name which certainly fits the description of hens and immature whiteface. Hens are charcoal grey with white suffusion on their faces in as much variation as one would see yellow suffusion on normal grey hens. The definitive white wing bar that appears on both sexes seems even brighter with all traces of yellow removed.

Whiteface chicks are identifiable immediately upon hatching because their down is white, regardless of the addition of any other colour or pattern change. Normal grey whiteface chicks have dark eyes, cinnamon whiteface chicks have plum eyes, and whiteface lutino chicks have red eyes.

This mutation was first reported in Holland in 1969.

In its early days in Australia the whiteface mutation suffered as a result of inbreeding to produce enough stock to develop the strain. For those breeders able to obtain birds, the general complaints were that some of the birds were small and poor in quality, nervous, difficult to pair for breeding and produced a high incidence of infertile eggs.

Right: Whiteface Lutino (albino). Bottom right: Whiteface Lutino Cinnamon - juvenile. Bottom left: Whiteface split Pied cock).

Subsequent generations have improved steadily in fertility and stability. Whiteface birds were combined with good normal birds and also the best available examples of feather pattern mutations, eventually producing some exceptionally beautiful birds of whiteface pearl and whiteface pied. By careful selective breeding we then added quality birds in colour mutations of lutino, cinnamon and silver. Only birds with a good background of size, conformation, temperament and fertility were used for these combinations.

Combination Mutations

While the whiteface in itself has caused a resurgence of interest in all things cockatiel, even more interesting is its effect on all other cockatiel mutations. The addition of the whiteface colour deletion allows breeders to produce new expressions of all the previously known colour changes; lutino, cinnamon, platinum, pastel silver, and fallow with no underlying yellow suffusion. Breeders easily combined the new double colour mutations such as whiteface cinnamon, etc., with the well established feather pattern alterations of pearl and pied. This quickly resulted in three and four visual mutations in a single bird, two of colour and one or two of pattern.

The normal grey whiteface is quite a stark bird in its formal contrasts of dark charcoal and white. When the pattern changes of pearl and pied are added the contrast is equally formal, and fascinating. The ideal whiteface pearl results from breeding the lovely heavily marked or lacewing pearl with whiteface. The result is a white ground bird with lacy charcoal pearls and only the faintest suffusion of grey on the bird's chest and abdomen. A whiteface pearl has predominantly white tail feathers with a fine black edging. Normal barring in juvenile or hen tail

feathers appears charcoal on a white background and the feather shafts are deep charcoal. Feet and toenails are grey toned but not as dark as normal grey whiteface. Whiteface pearl is a simple double combination of an autosomal recessive colour change and a sex-linked feather pattern change.

When whiteface pearl is combined with heavily marked pied the result is a beautiful white bird with small areas of lacy charcoal pearling on its shoulders. Heads and crests should be pure white regardless of sex because of the clear faced pied effect. These birds have dark eyes. Feet and toenails should have no colour. Clear faced pieds with fewer pied markings and, therefore, larger grey areas will be very attractive in this combination because more pearls will be visible. Whiteface pearl pied is a triple mutation combination.

Combining whiteface and lutino was the immediate goal for many breeders as this combination was to produce the true albino. With the whiteface preventing the production of any yellow and orange tones and lutino preventing any grey tones the resulting bird is bright white with red eyes. It is not a true albino but a multi-mutation. No amount of practical logic will prevent this white bird from being referred to as albino. However, I expect that some day we will have a spontaneous mutation that does produce albino without combining two mutations.

Albino cockatiels appear pure white with dark red eyes. Their feet and toenails are without any colour. If you want to breed albinos, take the time and effort to search out a very good lutino. In early combinations poor quality lutinos, such as those with bald spots, poor size and nervous temperament were used in some pairings. Several generations of careful breeding will be needed to breed the same strong qualities into the albino that we expect, and should demand, from our lutino birds. Lutinos, and therefore albinos, are not universally nervous, nor do they need to have poorly feathered heads.

To produce an albino you must have both parents carrying whiteface. In addition, the cock must carry lutino.

A suitable pairing would be a visual whiteface and a split whiteface with the cock also carrying genetics to produce lutino. Of his hen youngsters 50% will be lutino and 50% of all his offspring will be visually whiteface. Some of these colour genetics would quickly appear on the same young hen and you would see a whiteface lutino or your desired albino.

During the development of the cinnamon mutation we discovered when cinnamon and lutino were bred together brown colour remained on the bird. This was especially attractive when pearling was included.

When whiteface is added to this combination all yellow tones are removed from the lutino and cinnamon colours causing the bird to appear white with a cool brown colour washed over its shoulders, wings and tail feathers. Brown pearls are more obviously superimposed on its back and shoulders. This bird combines three colour changes and a pattern change as a whiteface lutino cinnamon pearl. I have no doubt this description will be quickly shortened to albino cinnamon pearl, which will be a total contradiction in terms, but may prove irresistible to use. Feet and toenails of this combination are colourless but its eyes are surprisingly dark red, a result of the cinnamon effect.

The second feather pattern of pied can be easily added to any of these combinations. Using pied birds with less, rather than more, pied markings will result in more areas of cinnamon colour on the white body of a whiteface lutino cinnamon pearl pied. This is a combination of three colour changes and two pattern changes. The bird may be easier to breed than it is to say its genetically honest name. This combination will probably be known as albino cinnamon pearl pied.

Secondary mutations of whiteface lutino, whiteface cinnamon, whiteface platinum, whiteface pastel silver, whiteface pearl and whiteface pied appeared within a few generations. Each combination has its own special merits and appeal.

When whiteface is combined with cinnamon the result is a softened brown tone with no yellow suffusion, giving a third colour effect to our cinnamon mutation. Hens carry little brown on their faces so when yellow is removed they have quite a white face. Cinnamon whiteface has been effectively combined with pattern changes. Cinnamon whiteface pearl, pied and pearl pied are stunning.

Whiteface platinum will produce a variable soft grey. Many platinum birds carry pearls and this will produce an even more softening effect.

Whiteface pastel silver, in my opinion, is more attractive than the normal pastel silver because all of the yellow tones are removed from the dilute colour. When combined with pearl it is a lovely bird. I expect whiteface silver pied and pearl pied to finally satisfy my mental image of a silver pied bird.

To achieve such ideal mutations selective breeding and further outcrossing to the finest cockatiels available is required to maintain the quality of the birds while improving their body markings. Breeding for size, conformation, fertility, feathering, temperament and natural parenting are all part of responsible selective breeding. Colour should be low on a list of priorities after the physical requirements listed before. In the rush to produce quantities of visual whiteface some inferior birds have been used in breeding. Careful breeding programs will produce perfectly marked pied and pearled birds just as we have in our normal grey or cinnamon birds.

Combining whiteface with fallow or the spangle silver would not add strength to any of the three mutations. The development of the whiteface cockatiel in Australia will go on for some years to come and if the emphasis remains on achieving birds of outstanding quality and beauty, their popularity should continue to grow and prosper.

Yellowface

The yellowface mutation is the latest mutation to be established in cockatiels. It is a typically strong sex linked mutation with no apparent loss of size or fertility when developed with responsible management.

The birds seen in these photographs appear to be normally coloured except that they lack orange tones on their faces. The cheek patch is not absent but has been changed to deep gold rather than orange. Mature cock birds surround the golden area with their usual vivid yellow in head and neck, thus producing the effect of a golden head. The hen also lacks orange tones which leave her face

Above left:
Yellowface cock.
Above right:
Yellowface hen
Opposite page:
Yellowface pair.

considerably more yellow than usual, even with the masking effect of grey melanin.

The grey body tones are the same as a normal wild type grey. The birds pictured have yellow suffusion throughout the rest of their bodies that penetrates the white wing bar, edging the white feathers with a fringe of yellow. The yellow suffusion appears to be no different from other normal or mutation birds with a strong yellow undertone. Cere, beak, feet and toenails all appear normal grey. Eyes are dark brown. Yellowface chicks have yellow down and dark eyes when newly hatched and cannot be identified until pin feathers cover the cheek patch area.

The yellowface mutation was established in Europe during the late 1980's. Birds were legally imported into the United States by 1992 and breeders soon combined yellowface with other mutations of established strength and fertility. They have been pleased with the results and have found no major fault or problem in breeding with yellowface.

Once the Australian yellowface has been developed in size, strength and numbers, combining the cheek patch colour change with other mutations will be eagerly pursued.

Combination Mutations

When yellowface is combined with lutino the two sex linked mutations produce a more yellow bird. The yellowface mutation primarily affects the cheek patch, changing it to gold instead of orange; and lutino removes all grey, the resulting 'golden headed' bird should be very attractive. The already established combinations of lutino with pearl, pied and cinnamon should be even more interesting with a golden face. The two sex linked mutations affect different areas of colour and feather.

Other than whiteface, all mutations display the charming cockatiel cheek patch of bright orange. All of these mutations can have the cheek patch colour altered, giving an overall effect of a golden head when the bird is fully mature. The yellowface variety affects a specific area that has not been changed by any of the other mutations. No problems of dominance should occur between this new mutation and any of the others.

As this new variety becomes more available singly and in combination keep in mind that no hen can be split for yellowface. Lutino yellowface or pied yellowface hens must look like lutino yellowface and pied yellowface. Cocks can appear lutino, pied or grey and carry yellowface as a hidden factor. To plan breeding results use the same pairings as one would to breed lutino pearl or pearl pied cockatiels.

Next!

If no other mutations appeared I could quite happily breed cockatiels for as long as I have left to do so without finishing all the combinations, in quality, that I already see in my mind. I doubt that I could ever breed each mutation to the highest degree of quality that we desire. Better to aim high and miss than aim low and easily hit the target!

Some of the changes that have been expected, and some that may be in development are as follows.

A melanistic cockatiel, where the melanin is so dark that the bird appears primarily black could appear.

Pastel blue birds have been described to me. A blue colour would need to involve a feather structure change but certain shades of silver with yellow suffusion and possibly, dark factors, could produce the illusion of blue tones.

References to a slate-blue cockatiel, obtained through selection, can be found in overseas literature. The cock has a yellow head, red cheeks and white wing bars. The hen is darker slate-blue, without any brown markings. This description could be derived from lovebird colour descriptions. Lovebird slate blue is their version of blue with two dark factors.

A black cockatiel with a yellow head, olive green colours on breast, wings and trunk. This mutation (a cock) was first bred by Mr F E Kaedig (Hannover, Germany). I don't have details of the dates involved. Possibly the optical impression of the olive green colour in the feathers is caused through the influence of extra black melanin; heavy suffusion of yellow combined with grey or black appears an olive green tone.

Black eyed white cockatiels have been casually described many times. Usually they have been defined more carefully as part of other mutations such as lutino or platinum.

The possibility of a single mutation to cause pure white, or albino, still exists.

Cockatiels have the capability to develop orange streaks during periods of stress. These marks can disappear without going through a moult. I think this capability could mutate to an orange bird.

The red eyed silver is known to breeders overseas. I believe that it will some day appear here.

Another mutation concerned with the cheek patch colour is under development in the UK. It is reported to be inherited in an autosomal recessive mode and changes the orange cheek patch to peach colour and the yellow face to pale lemon. This variety is being called pastel face.

If a variation of pearl developed so that only the feather shafts were coloured the birds would appear finely striped.

If you are interested in the perfect cockatiel in any colour or pattern available I wish you many breeding seasons of pleasant observation and rewarding pleasure in the enjoyment of your hobby.

Publishers Note

This title is published by Australian Birdkeeper who produce a wide and varied range of avicultural literature including the world acclaimed Australian Birdkeeper magazine - a full colour, bi-monthly magazine specifically designed for birdlovers and aviculturists. It is the intention of the publishers to produce high quality, informative literature for birdlovers, fanciers and aviculturists alike throughout the world. It is also the publishers' belief that the dissemination of qualified information on the care, keeping and breeding of birds is imperative for the total well-being of captive birds and the increased knowledge of aviculturists.

Nigel Steele-Boyce
Publisher/Editor -In-Chief
Australian Birdkeeper

Quality Publications from Australian Birdkeeper

- A Guide to Asiatic Parrots in Australia.
- A Guide to Neophema & Psephotus Grass Parrots.
- A Guide to Australian Long & Broad-tailed Parrots and New Zealand Kakarikis.
- A Guide to Rosellas.
- A Guide to Gouldian Finches.
- A Guide to Eclectus Parrots.
- A Guide to Cockatiels & their Mutations.
- A Guide to Pigeons, Doves & Quail.
- A Guide to Lories & Lorikeets.
- A Guide to Basic Health & Disease in Birds.

- Anthology of Birdkeeping/Special Edition One.

- Australian Birdkeeper Bi-monthly magazine.

For further information on any of Australian Birdkeeper quality products/publications write to:

Australian Birdkeeper
P.O. Box 6288,
South Tweed Heads,
NSW 2486 Australia.
or
Phone: (07) 5590 7777 Fax: (07) 5590 7130
Email: birdkeeper@birdkeeper.com.au
http://www.birdkeeper.com.au